Primary Curriculum

Teaching the Core Subjects

Also available from Continuum

Primary Curriculum – Teaching the Foundation Subjects, Rosemary Boys and Elaine Spink
Observing Children and Young People, Carol Sharman, Wendy Cross and Diane Vennis
Psychology and the Teacher, Dennis Child
Reflective Teaching 3rd Edition, Andrew Pollard
Teaching 3–8 3rd Edition, Mark O'Hara

Primary Curriculum

Teaching the Core Subjects

Edited by
Rosemary Boys and Elaine Spink

continuum

Continuum International Publishing Group

The Tower Building   80 Maiden Lane
11 York Road   Suite 704
London SE1 7NX   New York NY 10038

www.continuumbooks.com

First published 2008
Reprinted 2011

British Library Cataloguing-in-Publication Data
A catalogue record for this book is available from the British Library.

ISBN: 9780826488398 (paperback)

Typeset by Free Range Book Design & Production Limited
Printed and bound in Great Britain

Contents

Section 3 **Teaching Science**

Section 4 **Teaching Information and Communication Technology**

Notes on Contributors

Kate Blacklock

Kate's teaching experiences have seen her work in the United Kingdom and abroad, in roles that have included science coordinator and deputy headteacher. She has extensive experience in the delivery of support services for science and is currently a Leading Learning Adviser with Education Excellence.

Rosemary Boys

Rosemary Boys is a senior lecturer in the Institute of Education at Manchester Metropolitan University where she teaches English, special educational needs and teaching studies. Rosemary qualified and taught for many years in Australia but also has extensive experience in England, working as a primary teacher and advisory teacher for English. She has been involved in consultancy work for major publishers.

William Cooper

William taught in secondary and primary schools before moving into Initial Teacher Education. His main area of interest is the teaching of English but he also has expertise in teaching studies and drama. He was the recipient of the Distinguished Teacher Award from Manchester Metropolitan University in 2004.

Bob Davies

Bob is a senior lecturer in Primary Mathematics at Bath Spa University. He has extensive experience of initial teacher education and of the primary sector in England and Wales. Bob was the headteacher of three primary schools. He has worked in an advisory capacity for the National Curriculum Council and for North West Shropshire Education Action Zone.

Nick Easingwood

Nick is Principal Lecturer and Programme Leader for PGCE Initial Teacher Training at the Faculty of Education Anglia Ruskin University in Chelsford, Essex. He regularly teaches ICT and general professional studies to Primary and Secondary PGCE trainees, and he maintains regular contact with schools through visiting tham on their school placements. He has co-authored four books on the subject of ICT in the primary curriculum, as well as contributing chapters to several other publications.

Debbie Eccles

Debbie is Operations Director of Education Excellence, providing support services for schools nationwide. During her career in the primary sector she held a number of roles including science coordinator, deputy headteacher, teacher adviser for science and senior adviser. Debbie is the Primary Adviser for the Science Learning Centre in the North West and is a member of the ASE Primary Committee.

Russell Jones

Russell Jones is a senior lecturer in the Institute of Education at Manchester Metropolitan University. He has taught on primary education courses at four universities, from undergraduate level to PhD supervision. His publications are mainly in the fields of language teaching, children's rights, children's literature and contemporary issues for minority ethnic children.

Ian Sugarman

Ian Sugarman was a primary teacher in schools in London and Oxfordshire before becoming an advisory teacher for primary mathematics in Shropshire, where he developed an interest in writing books of curriculum ideas and devised some innovative items of maths equipment. He has served on various QCA committees and been involved in the production of in-service videos demonstrating the nature of children's mental calculation strategies. Currently teaching on the BA and PGCE courses at Manchester Metropolitan University, he has an interest in re-presenting his practical-based activities electronically for the interactive whiteboard.

Elaine Spink

Elaine is a senior lecturer in primary education for Manchester Metropolitan University and North West Regional Manager for the National College for School Leadership's Bursar Development Programme. Elaine was a primary teacher and teacher adviser for science before joining the university. She has worked in Indonesia and South Africa as a consultant for primary education/school management developments, and has published in the fields of science education and adult learning. She writes and delivers courses for the Science Learning Centre in the North West.

Susan Wright

Sue Wright is a senior lecturer in primary education at Manchester Metropolitan University. She is an early years specialist and teaches science and teaching studies on undergraduate, postgraduate and employment-based routes into teaching. Sue is a consultant for a publishing company, developing creative resources and providing national in-service training.

Introduction

You cannot teach anyone anything; you can only help them to find it within themselves.
Adapted from Galileo Galilei (1564–1642), Italian astronomer and physicist

This book is about the teaching English, mathematics, information and communication technology (ICT), and science. More specifically, it deals in *how* to teach those subjects, drawing on conceptions of pedagogy which are firmly grounded in research and practice. It is not about subject content per se, nor about the delivery of one particular curriculum.

The content of education within a national or state system always extends beyond the boundaries of a prescribed curriculum, and is not confined exclusively to subject demarcations. Our understanding of the word 'curriculum' needs to be broader than that suggested by the term 'national curriculum'. Nevertheless, the education system, certainly in England and arguably in many other parts of the world, has become more focused on formal curricula, with an emphasis on what teachers must teach and what children must be taught. The curriculum is 'content heavy' and this content is organized into separate subject 'boxes', for pragmatic as well as for educationally justified reasons. Thus, this book's section titles are immediately recognizable as the core subjects of the English National Curriculum (DfEE, 2000).

There have undoubtedly been advantages to having a National Curriculum in England: learning objectives have focused teachers' attention on what they want children to *learn*, rather than simply 'do'; assessment has been placed at the centre of learning and teaching; and the National Curriculum legislates for equality of access. But times are changing – when are they ever not? – and as we move further into the twenty-first century, new conceptions of what effective education looks like are forming. These are unlikely to be so content-driven. In the last decade, the rapid obsolescence of taught knowledge has become ever more apparent. It has been suggested that for 5-year-old children today, over 60 per cent of the jobs they will do as adults have yet to be invented (Barrett, 2006). How do we educate for such rapid change? Certainly not by transmitting facts and taking a 'jugs and mugs' approach to teaching, where the teacher fills the pupils with knowledge. There will of necessity be increased focus on skills development, on understanding how to access information and on lifelong learning.

We are also seeing a movement away from the subject boxes to more integrated approaches. For example, the Primary National Strategy in England aims for high standards obtained through 'a rich, varied and exciting curriculum' (DfES, 2003). Reviews of the primary curricula in Scotland, Wales and Northern Ireland are leading the way in delivering richness in learning through diversity in themes and approaches. With this greater breadth and increased teacher autonomy comes greater responsibility, to make the best possible decisions for the education of the children. However, the need for teachers to understand the principles of good practice in the individual subject components will remain.

Not only has there been an emphasis on knowledge content in primary education but also on certain subject areas at the expense of others. We know from the insistent voices of teachers, student teachers, parents and children (and from a growing body of research evidence) that teaching time and effort in England has been too narrowly focused on English and mathematics, limiting attention to other areas of learning. Reviews of education throughout the UK reflect a commitment to re-focus on over-arching themes and perspectives.

The chapters in this book discuss effective *teaching*: but what they are really concerned with is effective *learning*. Therefore, throughout the chapters 'learning and teaching' is the phrase of choice, because it places learning at the forefront of all we do. This also necessitates consideration of your role in relation to learning and teaching. Are you a facilitator, who 'enables other people to work in the way that suits them best' (Cambridge Online Dictionary)? Or are you 'one who instructs', the definition of a teacher? (op cit). Does this distinction matter? We believe it does, and that you must have thought through its implications for the ways in which you fulfil your professional obligations. The roles of a primary teacher are many and varied, but to view yourself as primarily a facilitator immediately creates greater possibilities. It frees you from the shackles (often imagined but no less powerful) of having to 'know everything', since you will be facilitating rather than instructing and it is your expertise in enabling learning to progress that will be of paramount importance, not the quantity of subject knowledge you possess.

Addressing the formal curriculum 'effectively' (and this notion will be explored in the chapters) is but a part of the broader education we seek to provide in schools. For this reason, each section considers elements of the subject that lie beyond the formal curriculum, identifying and analysing the contribution of the subject to wider development and the contribution of wider experiences to engagement with subject content and issues.

At the heart of government drives to raise standards of attainment in primary education lies a curriculum much greater than one nationally imposed. This diverse curriculum entitles all children to the knowledge, understanding, skills, values and principles of their communities, societies, countries and world.

Intended audience

This book is primarily intended for newly qualified teachers and for trainee teachers following undergraduate and postgraduate routes into the profession. However, by virtue of the fact that its purpose is for the reader to understand the principles underlying recommendations of practice, as well as to know what those teaching principles are and how to apply them, it will support all those who wish to improve their teaching of English, mathematics, ICT and science in primary schools.

The book inevitably emphasizes the English curriculum, since England is where its contributors are based and where they have garnered their expertise: but it also draws on practice elsewhere in the UK and on international perspectives and examples.

Structure

Each of the four subjects is addressed in its own section, which is split into three chapters (and no hierarchy of subjects is implied in the order of presentation). The first chapter in each section, entitled 'The Principles', provides context through a review of the subject's historical development, and asks you to consider the pedagogical principles that are fundamental to each core subject area. While some of the principles may seem generic, there are significant differences in methodologies that make each subject idiosyncratic, and these differences have an impact on our engagement with the subject.

The second chapter in each section, 'The Practice', is concerned with the practical aspects of learning and teaching in the subject. It makes links between the theories explored in the first chapter and their implementation in terms of planning, teaching and assessment. The recommendations made are founded upon accepted principles of good practice.

The third chapter in each section, 'Beyond the Curriculum', asks you to consider the richness that can be brought to each subject when opportunities are provided for children to learn beyond the confines of a statutory curriculum. This chapter recognizes and celebrates the opportunities now available to encourage a more holistic view of the core subjects, the value of inter-subjectivity and learning beyond the classroom.

Each chapter stands alone so that you may choose to focus on a specific subject but reading across the chapters reveals the inter-relatedness of methodologies. Non-sequential reading is possible – and encouraged.

Throughout the book, the chapters address *you*, rather than 'the reader', and seek to engage you in the issues and debates. The 'Pause to think' boxes encourage you to reflect on practice in relation to your own views and experiences. It is important not to underestimate the power of reflection; and as we move towards teaching becoming a profession in which practitioners continue to develop and to upgrade their qualifications to the point where most teachers will have a Masters degree, independent and self-directed analysis will become ever more significant. Those who excel will be teachers who successfully blend theory and practice, informed and constantly modified by reflection, asking, for example: Why am I doing this? What is the most appropriate theoretical framework? How does this relate to my professional context? What do I need to do to improve the outcomes for the pupils?

The boxes marked 'Case study' and 'Example' enable you to contextualize the information and to visualize applications, and challenge you to evaluate your own practice. In these examples, different voices are represented – those of teachers, students and children – in order to offer a broad perspective and to enable you to view situations from different angles.

Contributors

A shared philosophy is the foundation for this book. Building on that, each subject section reflects the particular nature of that subject and the individuality of the author. The contributors are all subject specialists with extensive experience of primary teaching and/or teacher education.

To conclude, we recognize that you are already a reflective practitioner, with a well-formed understanding of the basics of all of the subjects covered in this book. We hope, through your engagement with this text, to enable you to articulate your understanding of what to teach, how to teach, why to teach it and what the outcomes are for the children for each of the primary curriculum subjects considered here. This book seeks to support you in your further development. We wish you well in your professional life.

Rosemary Boys and Elaine Spink

References

Barrett, N. (2006), 'Creative Partnerships: Manchester and Salford.' www.ioe.mmu.ac.uk/cue/seminars/ BARRETT%20Urban%20seminar1.doc (Accessed July 2007).

Department for Education and Employment (1999), *The National Curriculum: Handbook for Primary Teachers in England*. London: DfEE/QCA.

Department for Education and Skills (2003), *Excellence and Enjoyment: A Strategy for Primary Schools*. London: DfES Publications.

Teaching English: The Principles

Rosemary Boys

Chapter Outline

Teaching English gives you the legitimate opportunity to engage with kids books without being rubbished.

(Year 3 Trainee English specialist)

Introduction

In this chapter we will examine the background issues related to the teaching of English. Knowledge of these issues will enable practitioners to confirm their recognition of the important role of English as a subject in its own right, and also as the subject that supports all other areas of the curriculum, and influences many aspects of life beyond the classroom and school environment. We will examine the historical development of the English curriculum and the theoretical context underpinning the way we currently teach English. This will enable us to recognize why issues related to the teaching of English have been, and continue to be, contentious. Without this understanding it is difficult for practitioners to engage in the debate surrounding the decisions that are made concerning their own practice.

While the legislative processes that are discussed here are specific to the English educational system, the historical routes have been similar in most countries in which English is the main language. The theories that have informed the use of the different teaching models are also common to these different educational systems.

Within this chapter the subject 'English' is that area of the curriculum that recognizes and teaches the four modes of communication: speaking and listening (oracy), and reading and writing (literacy).

The place of English in the primary curriculum

While it is easy to become immersed in the content and pedagogy of the teaching of English, it is also important to remember why we teach it, and the relevance of being an effective user of oracy and literacy. However, asking any group of teachers *why* we teach English is a sure way to produce furrowed brows. This is obviously not because they are unaware of the answer, but rather because they are bemused by the seeming naivety of the question. Yet it is a question that should be reflected upon in order to remind ourselves of the significance of the subject.

Case study

During an in-service day for newly qualified teachers (NQTs), participants were asked to work in small groups, and list the four main reasons why they thought the teaching of English was so important. Although the reasons that were given were worded differently, they could all be reduced to eight basic statements. These were:

- so that teachers and children can enjoy reading, writing and their literate culture
- because effective communication is essential for social, emotional and academic development
- so that children will become competent literacy users
- because oracy and literacy are the basis of all learning
- to enable effective access to the whole curriculum
- because without communication skills you would be unable to function in society
- because society demands that all people in employment have appropriate oracy and literacy skills
- because we need an articulate and literate workforce to compete economically in the world.

It is evident that as practitioners teaching English our responsibilities range from educating individuals who enjoy reading and writing, to promoting the continuous cultural, social and economic welfare of society.

> **Pause to think**
>
> In the light of the case study, what do you consider to be the roles of government, educationalists, teachers and parents in educational decision making?

The historical development of English in the primary curriculum

Perhaps it is because of its wide-ranging role that of all of the subjects taught within the primary school curriculum, English is the subject that has historically engendered controversy that extends beyond the teaching community. This controversy is common to all English-speaking countries, with the disagreement focusing on both the content of the English curriculum and its pedagogy. The debate is often based on a perceived decline in the standard of literacy, and a remembrance of a 'golden age'. Lewis and Wray (2000) argue that comparing standards of literacy over time is notoriously difficult because of society's changing expectations and requirements. This can best be understood through an awareness of the historical context of the teaching of English. It should also be recognized that because of Britain's international and colonial roles during the nineteenth and early twentieth centuries, developments in the teaching of English in Britain has had influence beyond the country itself, particularly among other members of the British Commonwealth.

Although the children of the affluent and privileged members of society have long had access to education, the need for a universally literate society began with the Industrial Revolution. As Britain gained international ascendancy in manufacturing and commerce in the nineteenth century, the utilitarian need for a literate workforce was recognized. This resulted in the Elementary Education Act of 1870 (the Forster Act), which introduced the first compulsory, free school attendance laws for children between 5 and 12 years. While this seems commendable legislation, it must be remembered that the introduction of state-controlled elementary schools was for the benefit of the economy rather than because of concern for children. Classes were enormous, teachers were poorly trained and the reading and writing curriculum's main resources were religious and moral texts. The pedagogy was one of teacher dominance, which required children to be passive learners. Reading was taught by rote, and writing was concerned with copying text and penmanship rather than creative expression.

In primary and infant schools the move from rote learning and instructional skills to more active methods of teaching (Aldrich, 2003) was the outcome of the second (1931: Primary Education) and third (1933: Infant Education) reports of the Consultative Committee of the Board of Education (often termed the 'Hadow' reports after Sir Henry

Hadow, the chair of the committees). These committees were influenced strongly by the views of the American philosopher and educationalist John Dewey (1859–1952). Dewey (1956) believed that 'learning is active. It involves reaching out of the mind. It involves organic assimilation starting from within.' The acknowledgement of these principles meant that the second and third Hadow reports were recognized as the beginning of progressive education Britain. They also introduced the subject of 'English' with a recognizable structure and pedagogy.

The reports recognized that effective oracy skills are vital for children's social, emotional and cognitive development. The second report states that 'through language, children can transform their active questing response to the environment into a more precise form and learn to manipulate it more economically and effectively' (Board of Education, 1931: 22). It also recognized that effective reading and writing required the explicit development of children's oral skills, which were subsequently encouraged in infant classes.

Reading and writing were to be taught together, so the learning in one could support learning in the other. Reading was no longer taught for purely utilitarian purposes and the committee argued that older children should be encouraged to read 'for pleasure and information' (Board of Education, 1931: 158). The recommended teaching methodologies for reading were phonic decoding and word recognition. This acceptance of 'official' methodologies, together with the promotion of school libraries, led to the establishment and growth of publishing companies printing both primers and books catering for the wider reading requirements of children. Many of these published reading materials were adopted and used in other English-speaking countries, which ensured the ascendant position and reputation of the English system for teaching literacy for many years.

In 1967 the Report of the Central Advisory Council for Education (England) into Primary Education in England (the Plowden Report), which was entitled *Children and their Primary Schools*, was commissioned by the government in order to evaluate the quality of primary education in England and Wales. The recommendations it proposed were controversial, and the child-centred Piagetian theory underpinning the report was severely criticized by some psychologists and educationalists (Donaldson, 1978; Halsey and Sylva, 1987). The changes proposed to the English curriculum also led to debate by those antagonistic to the concept of progressive education. Twenty years after the report was published, Scruton (1987) still argued that the Plowden Report was responsible for 'the educational decline we have witnessed in recent years'. Despite this criticism, the philosophy of child-centred education was endorsed until the advent of the National Curriculum.

Plowden recognized that in the development of children's oral language 'correctness should be sacrificed rather than fluency, vigour or clarity of meaning' (DES, 1967: para 582). Drama and listening to and telling stories were also endorsed as means of developing both oracy and literacy. It was argued that 'spoken language plays a central role in learning' (1967: para 54), and that 'the complex perceptual-motor skills of reading and writing are based, in their first stages, upon speech and upon the wealth and variety of experience from which effective language develops' (1967: para 14).

With reference to the teaching of reading, the report found that 'the most successful infant teachers have refused to follow the winds of fashion or commit themselves to any one method' (DES, 1967: para 584). However, concern was expressed about the quality and content of the reading books used in all schools. In particular, it was the representations of middle-class family life as the norm that were questioned, and deemed inappropriate and irrelevant for children from less affluent circumstances. Plowden also reported that many schools had an inadequate number and range of books, and that libraries were under-resourced. It was argued that children needed access to good quality non-fictional books and poetry as well as narrative texts through which they could learn the 'value of story' (1967: para 597). One of the most significant recommendations made by Plowden was that schools in areas of social deprivation should be given extra resources to address this deficit.

In the development of writing, Plowden reiterated the value of children learning to read and write at the same time, and emphasis was placed on the need for composing texts, rather the decontextualized teaching of secretarial skills (spelling, formal grammar teaching and handwriting). It was argued that young writers should develop their writing skills by writing 'something that has really engaged their minds and imaginations' (1967: para 603). In the light of this philosophy the formal study of grammar was rejected, as it was considered appropriate that 'the use of language should precede attempts to analyse grammatically how language behaves' (1967: para 612).

When addressing the secretarial skills, Plowden stated that 'it was only when inaccuracy impeded communication that steps should be taken to remedy the deficiencies' (1967: para 602). Spelling was considered to be best taught informally and in conjunction with children's interest in words, their shape, sound, meaning and origin.

For much of the twentieth century the English system of teaching English through a child-centred, progressive system was observed and emulated by the rest of the English-speaking world. However, while the Bullock Report on English (DES, 1975) endorsed and confirmed this practice, the combined effects of some dissenting educationalists, pressure groups calling for a return to 'basics', and the national need for financial stringency saw the beginning of a move away from innovation in the teaching of English. In November 1988 Kenneth Baker, the Secretary of State for Education for the Government of the United Kingdom, published the proposals for a National Curriculum for English. Following a consultation process (the DES and Welsh Office, 1989 Cox Report) that informed the final curriculum requirements, the National Curriculum for English was published, and introduced into primary schools in England and Wales in 1990.

While education in other English-speaking countries had long been subject to a mandatory, content-based English curriculum, the advent of a national curriculum for the teaching of English was revolutionary in the English and Welsh educational systems.

A theoretical framework for the teaching of oracy, reading and writing

To be successful in the acquisition of literacy, children need mastery of all four modes of language. As well as competence in speaking and listening, beginning readers also need to enjoy books, and to be familiar with their basic characteristics through shared reading with an adult. This familiarity will provide children with an awareness that print is meaningful, an understanding of print concepts, and the ability to recognize letters and words in a written context. While having only 26 letters to express approximately 44 phonemes (depending on your accent) presents irregularities within our phonic system and problems for phonic decoding, word recognition and spelling, it is now recognized that becoming literate is more than the development of phonic decoding/encoding skills.

Oracy acquisition

Competence in oracy has long been acknowledged as a prerequisite for reading and writing (Browne, 2001; Grudgeon et al, 2005). Medwell et al (2005) confirm this and further argue that 'talk is central to the primary curriculum…encouraging children to listen carefully and become confident speakers in a wide range of different contexts will provide them with a strong foundation for communication in its broadest sense'(p. 112).

But should we only be recognizing the role of speaking and listening as a contributor to academic success? The DfES (2003) also consider that a child's competency in speaking and listening is vital to their social relationships, their confidence in the classroom and their attitude to learning. As primary practitioners charged with the development of the child academically and socially, emotionally and behaviourally, the continuous and explicit modelling and interactive teaching of speaking and listening is essential.

Case study

Jack began his schooling in Year 1 just two weeks after his fifth birthday. As his family had moved during the summer holidays he knew none of his classmates, nor had he been able to visit his new school before the new academic year began. However, he had been looking forward to starting 'big school', and arrived full of quiet enthusiasm.

Before school began Jack's mother spoke with the class teacher. She was concerned because Jack was shy in new and unfamiliar surroundings, and explained that when he began in the nursery it took him several weeks to begin interacting with the other children or participating in the activities. She also handed the teacher Jack's developmental records from his nursery.

Case study (continued)

During registration Jack was introduced to the class. The teacher admired his new uniform, and asked Steven, a quiet child not unlike Jack, if he would be Jack's special friend for his first few days. Over the first few days Jack was very quiet, but with encouragement he began to participate more actively. Steven and Jack became good friends and began to visit each other's homes after school. The liaison between Jack's teacher and his mother was maintained.

Several days after his arrival Jack's new classmates began to notice that his accent was different from theirs. Their teacher explained all about accents, and asked them to think of all of the other people they knew who had accents different from their own.

This case study had a positive outcome, but it was not the result of serendipity. As well as having a proactive mother Jack also had an excellent teacher. She used the information provided by Jack's mother, and was aware that:

- Jack was very young, and consequently still acquiring and fine tuning his oral language and metalinguistic skills.
- He was upset by the disruptions in his home life and grieving over the absence of his extended family.
- From his file, she knew that although a quiet child, Jack's oral language was developing well. By using this information to inform her own planning and assessment she was able to ensure that his progress continued.
- Jack had an accent that was significantly different from the other children in her class. This could have an impact on her teaching of grapho-phonic relationships, and also make Jack feel different, vulnerable and unwilling to participate in discussions.
- Steven and Jack's friendship would provide both children with opportunities to practise using their developing oracy skills beyond the classroom.

In another context and without the information provided by his mother the outcome for Jack could have been different. Despite a growing recognition of the value of diversity in spoken language, there are still those who would make judgements about a child's intelligence and social status on the basis of how they speak. Being a quiet child with a strong regional accent, assumptions could have been made about Jack that could have resulted in a quite different provision for him.

Learning to speak and listen effectively in your first language is the most difficult learning task ever undertaken, and effective oracy acquisition is as much a social process as one of cognition. The ability to use oral language competently is a resource that children bring into school and that is often taken for granted (Grudgeon et al, 2005), and many adults still consider oral language acquisition to be an issue only in the teaching of young children. Effective practitioners, however, recognize that learning to use oral language well in different contexts, and for different purposes, requires continuous modelling, teaching and practice throughout the primary school, and beyond. Mukherji and O'Dea (2000) support this, and argue that 'the degree to which (oracy) skills are encouraged and nurtured will have a profound effect on their education, social and emotional success' (p. 67).

Theoretical models of reading

> **Pause to think**
>
> Consider how you learned to read, and the texts you read. Who first made you aware of print, and what kind of print was this? Was it at home or at school? Was it a positive

The bottom-up models

The historical models of reading that have been discussed so far have been those which assumed that the process of reading involved using a series of decoding skills. These progressed from the recognition of the lower levels of print (letters/graphemes and words) to reading simplified sentences and finally comprehension skills. The teaching approach to these models was based upon the careful and explicit teaching of word recognition, phonological skills, grapho-phonic knowledge and sound blending. These were often taught without a meaningful context for the young learner. The books used specifically to teach reading using bottom-up models tended to have controlled language, short sentences and little variation in the text structures. As the illustrations rarely supported the text, there was little semantic support for young readers to use. While these books supported most children as they learned to read, it was difficult for them to engender a love of reading or a passion for books. The genres of texts that were used were mainly fictional, with little or no use of non-fiction.

Examples of these models include the Phonics model, Look and Say, and the Skills-based model.

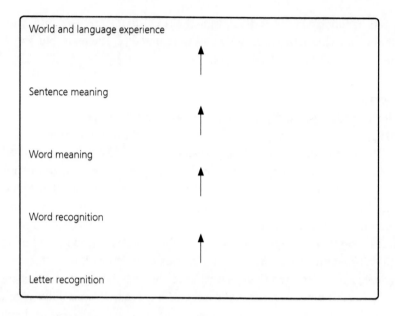

Figure 1.1 The bottom-up model of teaching reading

All Phonic models depend on the development of children's auditory skills, as children are required to identify sounds in spoken words (phonological awareness) and blend these into words for reading. Effective auditory skills (memory, perception and discrimination) are all necessary so that children can distinguish between sounds and hear rhymes. Children with poor auditory skills or hearing difficulties will find this a difficult system through which to learn to read.

The Look and Say model is based on the recognition of whole words. These are often taught through the use of word cards, Pelmanism and matching games. The skills to be taught in this model rely upon the use of visual memory, perception and discrimination. Children who are not strong visual learners will find this a difficult way to learn to read.

With both of these models comprehension can be problematic, particularly if children have had limited experiences with books. Because children focus on word-by-word decoding of the text there is no reference to either the meaning of what is being read, or the use of their knowledge of sentence structure to support understanding.

During the 1960s and 1970s the Skills-based model was developed, and used extensively in both the USA and Australia. It was a model that was strongly marketed and promoted by the publishers of educational resources. This model combined the systematic and rigorous teaching of the individual skills of both the phonic and word recognition models. As well as developing specific reading books, the schemes that supported the Skills-based model also included handbooks, tests and assessment checklists for teachers, and activity sheets and workbooks for children. These 'activities' were based on the texts, but focused on the development of one particular decoding skill.

The top-down model

The top-down model of reading emerged in the early 1980s in the USA, Canada, Australia, New Zealand and Britain, and was termed the psycholinguistic or whole language approach. Unlike the deficit-based bottom-up models that tended to be endorsed by research examining why children *can't* read, this model was based on research examining how successful early readers learn to read. It is a model that argues that, right from the start, reading is a process that places emphasis on meaning-making, and that children use the same range of strategies to gain meaning as adults. The model recognizes that the process of learning to read should have a social dimension, be enjoyable, and use real books (Goodman, 1967; Smith, 1978). By using their prior experiential knowledge and linguistic knowledge (syntactic cues), and the meaning in the text (semantic and picture cues), it was found that even beginning readers could engage with the text. Phonic skills (grapho-phonic cues) and word recognition skills are taught within the context of the text or the story being shared, and strategies for decoding using the text are taught explicitly and collaboratively through modelling, demonstration and discussion between adult and child.

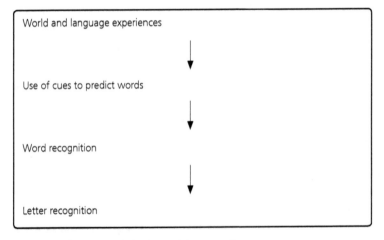

Figure 1.2 The top-down model of teaching reading

This model uses well-written and well-structured books that are relevant to children's ages and interests, and makes explicit use of their metacognitive and metalinguistic awareness. In England and Wales it was sometimes termed 'The real book method'.

The interactive model

This is a pragmatic, text-based model of teaching reading that is also based upon metacognitive and metalinguistic principles. The model recognizes reading as the active interaction between the reader and the text where a variety of strategies can be used. To provide children with the optimum opportunity for success they are *explicitly* taught all of the strategies and cues used by competent readers to gain meaning from text. The interactive literacy model is illustrated in Figure 1.3.

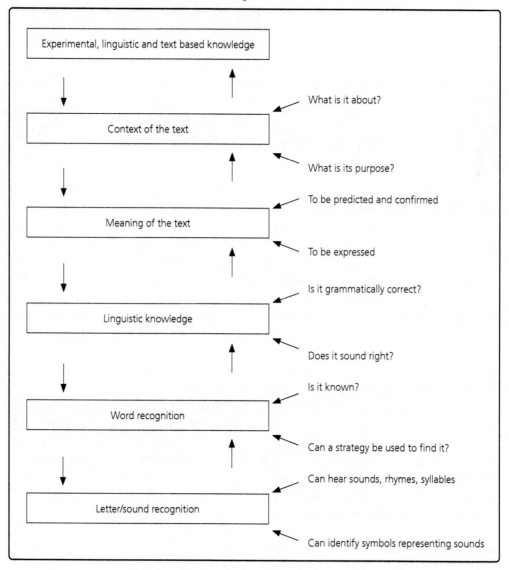

Figure 1.3 The interactive literacy model

However, as the figure indicates, while it strongly derives from the top-down model, this model also includes the rigorous and explicit teaching of print concepts, cueing systems and grapho-phonic knowledge, through the context of a well-written and structured text. It is also currently recognized that for beginning readers the systematic teaching of phonemic awareness may be taught separately.

This model's reference to textual features, and its recognition that reading and writing inform each other, make it an appropriate model for the explicit, genre-based teaching (EDWA, 1994a, 1994b) that is now a strong feature of the English curriculum in most English-speaking countries.

The model requires the use of well-written and genre-specific fiction and non-fiction texts. As shared reading (a methodology developed by Holdaway in the late 1970s) is extensively used in this method, big books (and most recently books on DVD) have become a common feature of literacy lessons.

The development of writing methodologies

To a large extent the development of formal writing methodologies has followed that of reading methodologies. As reading methodologies moved their focus from decoding letters and words to a model recognizing the significance of meaning and linguistic experience, so writing also moved from encoding letters into words to recognizing the importance of composing.

As with reading, research into writing acquisition is becoming concerned with the influences and understandings affecting the writing development of young children. Until recently, there was little theoretical evidence of such development in very young children, and the collection of valid evidence to distinguish between drawing and writing has been methodologically problematic. However, the work of Lancaster (2007) and Harris (2000) shows that, in their mark-making, children as young as 18 months indicate a systematic desire to communicate, and that such mark-making has evidence of graphical and semantic awareness and elements of grammaticization (Langacker, 2000).

Early childhood teachers are aware of the role of mark-making in the development of writing. Consequently, most children who have had well-informed Early Years education will have experienced opportunities to engage in 'play' writing. This will have been generated by contexts designed to promote and extend all of the above understandings (Hall and Robinson, 1995). They will also have had opportunities to continue to develop the fine-motor skills essential for writing.

On entering the primary school, children should that know that writing is:

- purposeful – they have seen adults writing lists, labels and messages
- a way of communicating – they have seen adults writing notes, letters, texts and emails

- organized differently – they have seen bills, adverts, labels, instructions, recipes and cards
- permanent – as the stories in their books stay the same.

However, in primary schools, while it is recognized that the whole purpose of writing is to communicate through written symbols, concern that writing is readable gains importance. Vygotsky (1978) recognized that 'children should be taught written language, not just the writing of letters' (p. 119). However, getting this balance between the *composing* (the meaning component) and the *secretarial skills* (spelling, grammar and handwriting) of writing has always been problematic (Grainger, 2005). This is particularly so with spelling, where the problem of having 44 phonemes and 26 graphemes requires systematic teaching of grapho-phonic relationships and skills in blending sounds together.

As with the teaching of reading, the teaching of writing has progressed from decontextualized, traditional methods to a model that focuses on the processes involved in writing. The explicit teaching of the different genres and forms of writing has enabled teachers to provide children with purposeful opportunities to explore the meanings, language and structures of texts at all levels of the primary school (Riley and Reedy, 2000; Hall, 1999).

Change has also taken place in the way children's writing is assessed. Recognition should now be given to children's awareness of the idiosyncrasies of the different purposes and forms of text, the meaning component of the child's writing, and the positive evidence of the development of secretarial skills. No longer should children's writing be devalued by an enthusiastic red pen.

Principles of good practice

As practitioners, we recognize the complexities in the teaching of English. But despite this, there are aspects of the teaching of English for which we as committed professionals must accept responsibility. These include:

- sharing a genuine enthusiasm for written and spoken language with the children we teach
- keeping abreast of new authors and publications that will enhance our teaching
- providing a print-rich learning environment within the classroom, which includes texts written by the children, and promotes discussion, reading and writing
- developing an understanding of the language needs and strengths of the children we teach
- providing learning tasks that are enjoyable, purposeful and relevant to the children
- maintaining and updating our subject knowledge, and awareness of current research and newly developed resources (especially in ICT)
- establishing purposeful and mutually respectful relationships with parents and carers.

Conclusion

In this chapter we have considered briefly the historical and methodological development of the teaching of English. The two most consistent features of this development have been the controversy and changes that have taken place. Both of these continue into the contemporary teaching of English agenda. You will be aware of concerns centred around boys and their reluctant engagement with literacy, the moves by some educationalists to promote and increase the significance of synthetic phonics into the English curriculum, and the increasing demands of inclusion on our practice. As practitioners it is important that we engage and participate in these debates. To do this with confidence,practitioners need knowledge of not just 'how' to teach this subject, but also of the theoretical and methodological implications of any decisions made.

References

Aldrich, R.A. (2003), *A Century of Education*. London: Routledge.

Board of Education (1931), *The Primary School*. London: HMSO.

Board of Education (1933), *Infant and Nursery Schools*. London: HMSO.

Browne, A. (2001), *Developing Language and Literature 3–8*. London: Paul Chapman.

Department for Education and Skills (2003) *Excellence and Enjoyment: A Strategy for Primary Schools*. London: DfES.

Department of Education and Science (1967), *Children and their Primary Schools*. London: HMSO.

Department of Education and Science (1975), *A Language for Life*. London: HMSO.

Department of Education and Science and the Welsh Office (1989), *English for Ages 5–6*. York: National Curriculum Council.

Dewey, J. (1956), *Child and the Curriculum and the School and Society*. Chicago: Phoenix Books.

Donaldson, M. (1978), *Children's Minds*. London: Fontana.

Education Department of Western Australia (EDWA) (1994a), *First Steps: Reading*. Melbourne: Rigby Heinemann.

Education Department of Western Australia (1994b), *First Steps: Writing*. Melbourne: Rigby Heinemann.

Goodman, K.S. (1967), 'Reading: A psycholinguistic guessing game.' *Journal of the Reading Specialist* 6,126–35.

Grainger, T. (2005), 'Motivating children to write with purpose and passion' in P. Goodwin (ed.), *The Literate Classroom*. London: David Fulton.

Grudgeon, E., Dawes, L., Smith, C., and Hubbard, L. (2005), *Teaching Speaking and Listening in the Primary School* (3rd edition). London: David Fulton.

Hall, N. (1999), *Interactive Writing in the Primary School*. Reading: Reading and Language Information Centre, Text Matters, University of Reading.

Hall, N. and Robinson, A. (1995), *Exploring Writing and Play in the Early Years*. London: David Fulton.

Harris, R. (2000), *Rethinking Writing*. London: Athlone.

Holdaway, D. (1979), *The Foundations of Literacy*. Auckland: Ashton Scholastic.

Lancaster, L. (2007), 'Representing the ways of the world: How children under three start to use syntax in graphic signs.' *Journal of Early Childhood Literacy*. 7 (2).

Langacker, R.W. (2000), *Grammar and Conceptualisation*. Berlin and New York: Walter de Gruyter.

Lewis, M. and Wray, D. (2000), *Literacy in the Secondary School*. London: David Fulton Publishers.

Medwell, J., Wray, D., Minns, H., Griffiths, V. and Coates, E. (2005), *Primary English: Teaching Theory and Practice* (2nd Edition). Exeter: Learning Matters.

Mukherji, P. and O'Dea, T. (2000), *Understanding Children's Use of Language and Literacy*. Cheltenham: Stanley Thornes.

Riley, J. and Reedy, D. (2000), *Developing Writing for Different Purposes: Teaching about Genre in the Early Years*. London: Paul Chapman.

Rowe, D. (1993), *Preschoolers as Authors*. New York: Hampton Press.

Scruton, R. (1987), 'Expressionist Education.' *Oxford Review of Education*. 13 (1).

Smith, F. (1978), *Understanding Reading*. New York: Holt, Rinehart and Winton.

Halsey, A. H. and Sylva, K. (1987), 'Plowden: History and prospect.' *Oxford Review of Education*. 13 (1).

Vygotsky, L. S. (1978), *Mind in Society: The Development of Higher Psychological Processes*. M. Colt, V. John-Steiner, S. Scribner and E. Souberman (eds and trands). Cambridge, MA: Harvard University Press. (Original work published in 1934.)

2 Teaching English: The Practice

Rosemary Boys

I have a 2:1 degree in English, but had no idea how to teach it. Having good subject knowledge is only part of the knowledge and understanding you need to help children become literate.
(PGCE trainee after completing their first placement)

Introduction

In Chapter 1 we considered why we need a literate population, and examined some of the theories underpinning the pedagogy for teaching English. In this chapter we will focus on how we endeavour to produce not only literate children, but children who value and enjoy their literate state. As teachers of English in the twenty-first century, our responsibility has moved beyond the utilitarian teaching of English to the education of children for whom literacy is enjoyable, purposeful and positive.

It is not the remit of this chapter to investigate the more simplistic aspects of the teaching of English (such as the writing of single lesson plans), but rather to examine a more holistic view of literacy teaching appropriate to a beginning practitioner. To do this effectively requires a clear understanding of what constitutes 'an effective teacher of English'. This will recognize that our own understanding of the context of the learning and our own perceptions of ourselves as English teachers are as important as what we teach, how we teach and the resources we use.

Preparing to teach English

How would we recognize an effective teacher of English?

During your own experiences in primary schools you will have encountered teachers passionate about the teaching of literacy. These teachers share common characteristics despite the age group they might be teaching. As well as having a clear understanding of the knowledge, skills and learning processes involved in becoming literate, their classroom environments are inspiring, and the children they teach have opinions and thoughts about texts and language that they are willing, and able, to discuss with enthusiasm.

Case study

On entering the classroom of Sally Evans and her Year 4 children it is easy to see what the children have been learning. Their classroom displays show the ways in which Sally has used other subjects to provide purposeful contexts for developing an understanding of the different genres of texts she is required to teach. At present the children's writing includes the instructions they used to make different kinds of puppets, the play scripts they wrote to enact their own fables, and alphabetically-ordered illustrations of everyone's fable characters.

The structured play area contains a puppet theatre where children can perform their fables using their puppets. There is a literacy corner that has books and audio books thoughtfully selected and presented to entice and engage young readers, and a wall display of book reviews that were written by the children, which is constantly changed by the children themselves as they extend their personal reading. This corner also has supplies of paper (some of which is stapled or folded into little blank books), different writing implements, dictionaries and thesauruses, so that children always have access to resources to support their independent writing.

The children enjoy talking about their favourite books. Dan thinks that Ms Evans enjoys reading children's books because she reads them during sustained silent reading (SSR) time, and if she enjoys them she reads them to the whole class in story time. He also thinks that her favourite poet is Benjamin Zephaniah, because she has put two of his poems into their class anthology.

The children in this class are aware that their teacher enjoys reading and writing herself. The teacher and children share the memories, experiences and language of books shared and enjoyed together.

> ### Case study (continued)
>
> When Dan and his friend Jack are asked if they enjoy writing they proudly retrieve their play script from the display, and explain that they both have really good ideas for writing, but that good writing takes a lot of thought and time. However, they both agree that: 'When we work together we can talk about the best words and where to put full-stops and things, and if we need help Ms Evans will help us, or let Mrs Kaur [the Teaching Assistant] work with us.'

As these children have recognized, the process of becoming literate is complex. To be an effective teacher of English requires an excellent understanding and knowledge of English, its pedagogy and the curriculum at the national, school and class levels.

Effective teachers have a profound impact on the literacy ethos of a school, and their influence will usually extend beyond their own classroom. For beginning teachers and trainees, such professionals make excellent role models.

What we need to know before we start teaching

The use of the curriculum and policy documentation

Most English-speaking countries have a mandatory English curriculum, which specifies the content, concepts and skills to be taught over a given period of time. In England it is the responsibility of each school to develop a policy that will enable teachers to implement this curriculum in the way that best fits their school's unique needs. An effective English policy must support continuity of provision, progression in learning, and coherence in planning and assessment for speaking and listening, reading and writing.

English policy documents should refer to organizational and pedagogical aspects of literacy teaching relevant to all English teaching within the school. For instance, this might include the requirement to use specific teaching methodologies, assessment requirements, or even the letter formation to be used in the teaching of handwriting.

As professionals we have a responsibility to participate in the writing and revision of school-specific English policies, as these are the documents that will regulate our everyday practice in planning, teaching and assessing the subject.

The school context

The impact of the school context on the organization and implementation of the English curriculum should never be underestimated. Whereas children were once expected to fit into the requirements of the school, schools now recognize the role of inclusive practices and seek to address the needs of the children in the communities they serve.

The school context can be influenced by its geographical area, the socio-economic level of the community it serves, the cultural diversity of the community and a range of other specific characteristics that can influence the English provision required for its children. This may have an impact on the way that classes are organized. For example, large schools may decide to put children into sets for English. This means that teachers will not have the same range of ability to teach, but will still be expected to differentiate learning. Teachers here are also likely to be able to plan collaboratively with colleagues. Conversely, in small schools teachers may be required to teach several year groups, resulting in the need for very thoughtful differentiation, that might be based on ability rather than age. As practitioners you will be aware of the implications of teaching both a wide age range and a wide ability range in a subject as complex as English.

With the advent of inclusive practices, and the introduction of the 'Every Child Matters' agenda (DfES, 2004), there has been increased recognition of the need for multi-professional working practices, and the provision of early intervention procedures for children with language and literacy problems. Schools and teachers need to understand how to access this support, and use it effectively.

School context will also influence staffing. In areas with a high percentage of minority ethnic children for whom English is an additional language (EAL), it is important that bilingual staff members are appointed. This is not just to support children learning English, but to ensure that children maintain and develop their first language, to liaise with parents and to contribute to the school's multicultural development.

Knowledge of children

To address the language and literacy needs of their class, teachers need to know a great deal about each child. Information is available from sources including children's records, reference to other colleagues and discussions with parents.

To differentiate English learning and teaching appropriately, teachers need to be aware of each child's attainment in each of the four modes of language. Teachers also need an understanding of any individual learning issues a child might have. This could include gifted children, those who have EAL, or those who have been identified as having a special educational need (SEN). All children have the potential to contribute positively to the richness and diversity of the English curriculum.

The children's home literacy environment also needs recognition, to ensure continuity between school and home where possible. Knowledge that a child's parents have poor English skills should result in alternative arrangements being made for the child to share their reading book with someone at school, and written homework could perhaps be supervised in a homework club. Children with EAL should have books available in their first language to take home and share.

Subject knowledge

To teach English effectively and confidently, teachers need to be secure in their subject knowledge. Planning, teaching and assessing all require a clear understanding of the subject matter to be learned. Without excellent subject knowledge it is difficult for teachers to extend the more able children, or identify and address any misconceptions or language needs that children may have.

Because of the importance of English in the curriculum, it needs to be recognized that English subject knowledge is not value free, and changes in subject content requirements do occur. While some of the changes are the result of rigorous, peer-reviewed research, other changes are the outcome of political decisions based on the lobbying of people who reject the current curriculum content. An example is the reintroduction of the decontextualized teaching of phonics. Competent teachers, particularly those teaching younger children, recognize the importance of phonemic awareness and grapho-phonic knowledge. They teach analytical and synthetic phonics rigorously and systematically through the context of texts. They are aware that the context of a text gives purpose to the learning of phonics and the development of auditory and visual skills. Schools and teachers have a responsibility to recognize which changes are significant and which are merely band-wagons.

ICT now has increasing relevance in the teaching of literacy. Rudd and Tyldesley (2006) recognize that literacy is now both paper and screen based, and that skills such as finding information, critical thinking, evaluative skills and the ability to re-present information in different ways for different audiences now need to be taught in order to develop children's competence in both forms of media. Contemporary communication systems such as e-mailing, texting, and website creation are also impacting on the English curriculum, and must be recognized as valid subject matter. It is therefore a requirement of teaching that we continuously maintain and extend our subject knowledge throughout our professional lives.

Knowledge of how to manage other adults

Currently the role of the teaching assistant (TA) is an active one, working with children and teachers to support learning and teaching. A survey of the management of TAs in schools (DFEE, 1999) recognized that effective practice by TAs should enable them to:

- foster the participation of pupils
- enable pupils to become more independent learners
- help raise the standards of achievement for all pupils.

Many TAs now have specific training, giving them both the status and qualifications to supervise classes, and to plan and assess lessons. It is also envisaged that in the future larger numbers of teaching assistants will be employed, and that the teacher's role will increasingly involve their supervision.

For many beginning teachers, managing such colleagues can be daunting. However, despite the status and responsibilities given to TAs, it is qualified classroom teachers who are accountable and responsible for the learning and teaching of the children in their care, and the management of other adults. To establish a working relationship for the effective support in English you will need to be aware of a TA's knowledge and experiences in the teaching of English. For example: Have they participated in collaborative planning and assessment? Do they have sound subject knowledge? Are they able to support groups of children? Are they familiar with the school's English resources? The ways in which TAs can be used to support children's learning in English are diverse and will vary depending on the lesson being taught.

Effective management of TAs in English lessons requires thoughtful planning, which is best done in collaboration with the TA involved. TAs can only provide support for your English lesson if they are well informed, and have a clear understanding of the lesson's objectives, and the expected outcomes for the children with whom they are working.

Knowledge of the teaching process

Coherent and well-informed English teaching can only be achieved through the effective implementation of the planning/teaching/assessing cycle. This cycle depends on the practitioner recognising that:

- a strong literature, language and comprehension programme includes a balance of oral and written language
- skills and strategies must be taught explicitly to develop children's metacognitive and metalinguistic awareness
- in genre-based programmes, other subjects must provide a meaningful context for specific genres
- planning must ensure coverage, progression and appropriate sequences of text/genre-based units
- interactive and differentiated lessons enable all children to participate successfully at their own level
- familiarity and knowledge of resources promotes interest and enhances learning
- teaching and assessment strategies support interactive lessons based on effective knowledge of children's understanding and attainment
- ongoing formative and diagnostic assessment will inform future planning.

Planning

Developing effective planning

Effective planning makes the curriculum accessible to children and provides continuity and progression in learning. This is achieved through three stages: long-term, medium-term and short-term planning. The quality of planning will influence the purposefulness of the lesson and children's engagement and enjoyment.

Long-term planning

Long-term planning provides an overview of English teaching for each term or semester of the year. It is not detailed but should indicate where the links between English and other subject areas will be made. It is at this level that purposeful contexts in other subjects will be identified for the teaching of different textual genres.

Figure 2.1 shows the collaborative long-term planning of two Year 4 teachers for one term. The following two terms would be planned at the same time. From this example it is possible to see the impact English planning has on the planning of other subjects, and gives some indication of their integration into English.

English	Maths	Science	ICT	History	Geog.	Art & Design	Physical education	PSHE and citizenship
Term 1								
Historical stories and short novels			Gathering data	Local study	Changes in the local area	Local buildings		
Playscripts			Word processing					
Poems based on common themes			Publishing for anthology	Collecting local poems or favourites of local people				
Recounted texts			Audio and video recording	Oral history from local people				
Instructions							Collecting and using games and their rules	Collecting and using local recipes

Figure 2.1 Long-term planning for a term

This level of planning should ensure coverage of the curriculum and enable the teacher to plan a coherent programme of learning.

Medium-term planning

Medium-term planning should cover teaching content for each term or half-term (or semester or half-semester). It is used to develop two or three week units of work into coherent sequences of lessons. At this stage the focus is placed upon the genre-appropriate texts and other resources that will be used, the areas of attainment that need addressing, and generalized learning objectives (that can be taken directly from English curriculum documents).

English units of work usually focus on reading first, and then writing. This enables children to develop a specific understanding of each form of text through reading and exposure to appropriate genre-specific texts. It provides children with the knowledge and skills that will inform their own writing – both composing and their secretarial skills. At this stage teachers give careful consideration to the sequencing of lessons, and the ways in which the learning and teaching will be organized.

Short-term planning

Unlike the single lesson short-term plans used during teacher training, the short-term plans used by practitioners are working documents that will give detailed planning for the unit, and provide an overview of each week and each daily lesson. In short-term planning it is important that general objectives from medium-term planning become precise single lesson learning objectives. Daily learning objectives will inform each aspect of the lesson, and also inform the learning outcomes that will be assessed during, or after, each lesson. At this stage a lesson will also include:

- whole class work
- differentiated work
- iInvolvement of other adults
- resources used
- learning outcomes
- assessment information.

Short-term plans are working documents that may be subject to changes. For instance, non-attainment on the previous day or a misjudging of children's prior knowledge are just two complications that might necessitate a modification. Consistent use of short-term planning and assessment will provide evidence of progression.

The use of ICT in the planning process

Samples of medium- and short-term planning for most English curricula are now available online, and many schools use these as the basis for their English planning. As no two schools have exactly the same curriculum requirements, these will need modification and adjustment. Teachers may also find that the continued use of downloaded plans erodes their ownership of planning and stifles their creativity. As professionals you will have to make decisions that will enable you to balance expediency and autonomy.

Strategies for teaching English

Teaching strategies promote and enhance the teaching process, especially children's engagement and inclusion. The implementation of these strategies is subject specific. While they promote children's engagement, they are not behaviour management strategies.

Scaffolding learning

Through scaffolding (Bruner, 1966), a learner can develop new concepts and understanding by building on prior knowledge (other strategies that will be discussed in this section seek to promote this process). Scaffolding is not just the responsibility of the teacher and adults in the class: children who have had literacy, language and communication strategies modelled for them are also able to scaffold for each other. Paired scaffolding is particularly successful in such problem-solving tasks as decoding, spelling, structuring a text and punctuation. Scaffolding does not just provide children with understanding and knowledge, but with the means and skills to promote their own learning – a much more powerful attribute.

Modelling

Modelling is the term used to describe the demonstration of a skill or means of going about something (Mallett, 2002). In English lessons modelling is most frequently used during shared reading and writing. During this part of a literacy lesson it is the teachers' role to give explicit demonstrations of how strategies and skills are used. For example, shared reading with younger children could include the use of:

- *Prediction* – The reader makes an educated guess using their prior experiential understanding and knowledge.
  Teacher: 'Mmm, I wonder what will happen next?' 'What do you think Lucy?' 'What makes you think that?'

- *Picture cues* – The reader can use the semantic information in the illustrations to predict and decode individual words, especially nouns.
  Teacher: 'I think this word must be elephant. Look, here's the picture of an elephant, and the word begins with "e".'

- *Repetition* – Events, language and structure are often repeated in children's books. Once children recognize the repetition, they can predict the next episode.
  Teacher: 'The author seems to be repeating this sentence again. Can you help me read it?'

- *Intertextual skills* – Children need to know they can bring their knowledge of the structure and content of one book to their reading of another.
  Teacher: 'I think this story is very similar to "The Enormous Turnip". I wonder who will come to help next?'

- *Semantic cueing* – Words such as nouns, verbs, adjectives and adverbs can be read from the context of their sentence.
  Teacher: 'I think I will read past this word and think what would make sense.'

- *Syntactic cueing* – Words such as different parts of a verb (fly/flew), determiners, prepositions and connectives can be read from the grammatical context of their sentence.
  Teacher: 'I think I will read past this word and think: Which word would make the sentence sound right?'

- *Grapho-phonic cueing* – As children develop phonemic awareness and segmenting skills, they will recognize analogies they can use for decoding.
  Teacher:'I can segment and sound this word out.'

Modelling develops children's metacognitive and metalinguistic awareness, and encourages them to engage in active, self-motivated learning. It is essential in the development of spelling strategies, and enables children to structure and punctuate a written text using the skills modelled in shared writing.

Questioning

Through questioning we can purposefully promote children's speaking and listening skills, as well as promoting learning and teaching. Briggs et al (2003) argue that for children the aim of questioning should be to give 'give thoughtful answers rather than simply agree or disagree' (p. 34). This is supported by Headington (2000), who recognizes that questioning 'enables teachers to delve into children's thinking' (p. 26).

We have already considered how questions can be used to model and promote metacognitive and metalinguistic strategies. They can also promote learning by:

- engaging children's prior knowledge
- encouraging participation in discussions
- probing understanding and misconceptions
- encouraging predicting, reasoning and explanation
- encouraging children's own use of literal and inferential skills.

Once a teacher can use questioning effectively, it will also become one of their most effective tools for assessment.

Although there is pressure on beginning teachers to maintain pace in their English lessons, a balance is needed between pace and giving children time to think. To get the response you want it might be necessary to ask a series of questions, or use questions that probe and prompt thinking.

In English, where comprehension is important, teachers modelling literal, inferential and analytical questioning during shared and guided reading will support the development of children's own questioning skills. Similarly, being aware of questions used for synthesis (for example:'How could we make this sentence more descriptive?') will encourage a more reflective approach to the construction of texts.

Differentiation and inclusive practice

Differentiation is an inclusive strategy that enables teachers to give each child appropriate access to the curriculum. In English this is done through: the use of differentiated questions during whole class lessons; the use of ability groups; the support of an adult; or by having different levels of difficulty in tasks. Differentiation to address the needs of children with EAL or special educational needs has long been recognized. However, all children deserve relevant and challenging learning opportunities.

While it is important for children to work at their own level, the use of paired learning should also be considered, especially in writing. We have already recognized that children can successfully scaffold for each other, and opportunities for this should be created.

Use of resources

Children's ability in reading and writing different genres depends on their access to genre-appropriate examples of texts. Non-fictional texts that are age and genre specific are now available in big book form, on CD-ROMs and as resources for interactive whiteboards.

Good quality fictional books for younger children should include patterned, predictable texts with repetition, rhythm, rhyme and an interesting storyline to which children can respond. Such texts are easily accessible even in commercial reading schemes. However, even young children are entitled to engage more positively with the wonderful range of children's literature now available. These books are far more than resources to support reading development. Johnston (2001) argues that 'children's literature is an artistically mediated form of communication – a conversation – that society has with its young' (p. 329), and justifiably some authors object to their work being dissected and probed unrelentingly. As practitioners we must engage children with their reading heritage in creative and sympathetic ways (such as those addressed in Chapter 3).

Use of ICT

Currently much of the emphasis on ICT in English lessons focuses on the use of computers, software packages and interactive whiteboards. The quality of these and of the websites available to support English continue to develop, and provide excellent support for teachers. It is important, however, that we do not forget more familiar ICT resources. Audio and video equipment and digital cameras are also powerful means of engaging children in speaking, listening, reading and writing.

Assessing and monitoring progress in English

Browne (2001) maintains that standards in English are probably monitored more closely than other areas of the curriculum. However, while knowing that an 11-year-old child is reading at Level Four and writing at Level Three in national tests may be statistically useful in preparing the school's development plan, benchmarking schools and criticizing the teaching of English in the national press, it gives no information about an individual child's strengths or specific areas for development. Briggs et al (2003) define assessment as 'the process of finding out about what a child can do, and where there might be difficulties' (p. 5). It is therefore part of a continuous process that will provide teachers with both diagnostic information and evidence of attainment (or non-attainment) in lessons.

Assessment that informs teaching can be done independently of a lesson, or within it. Hall and Burke (2003) recognize that literacy is a complex subject, and there are many areas within it that need to be assessed. Figure 2.2 identifies the most significant of these.

Aspects to assess	Frequency	Method of assessment
Speaking and listening		
Articulation	Regularly	Observation
Speaking for different purposes	Specifically	Observation in other subjects
Communicating and conversing as appropriate to the context	Regularly	Engagement in talk observation
Recounting	Regularly Specifically	Observing Retelling stories events
Ask and respond to questions	Regularly Specifically	Engagement in talk Drama
Able to use Standard English as required	Specifically	Observation
Reading		
Print concepts	Regularly	Observation
Phonemic awareness	Regularly	Observation, questioning
Decoding strategies	Regularly Specifically	Observation, questioning Running record analysis
Comprehension	Regularly	Questioning, discussing, marking written tasks
Understanding of genre-specific texts	Regularly	Questioning, marking written examples of different genres
Writing		
Composition	Regularly	Discussion, marking, questioning
Writing of genre-specific texts	Specifically	Annotating written work, analysis
Grammatical awareness	Regularly	Discussion, marking
Language variety	Regularly	Discussion, marking
Punctuation	Regularly	Marking
Phonemic awareness	Regularly	Marking
Encoding (spelling) strategies	Regularly Specifically	Marking Discussion, questioning
Handwriting	Regularly Specifically	Observation Annotating written work

Figure 2.2 Opportunities for assessing aspects of English

Assessment within a lesson

The focus of this form of assessment is based on the learning objective and expected outcomes set for the lesson. To assess and monitor formatively and effectively, practitioners need to have a clear understanding of who, what and why they are assessing, the assessment strategies that can be used, and how they might use the information collected. Evidence of attainment and understanding will be based upon the effective use of:

- questioning
- observing
- discussion
- marking and analysing children's work
- children's self assessment.

To give evidence of progression in English, formative assessment (assessment for learning) must be ongoing, well planned, and recorded appropriately. The careful construction of assessment records will also inform target-setting for individual children, and serve as the basis for feedback to children and reports for parents.

One aspect of English that is often neglected is speaking and listening: yet this is the most essential mode of communication. However, because of the transitory nature of speaking and listening, its assessment can be problematic. To be relevant such assessments should be observed in different contexts: and therefore they can be done in any lesson that provides an appropriate context. For example, if asking and responding to questions is being assessed, then the hot-seating of an historical character could be used. Alternatively, for evidence that a child can orally explain, report and justify, a science lesson would be more suitable.

Providing constructive feedback

Feedback to children can be in oral or written form. If it is constructive, the feedback should 'scaffold' children's language and literacy development, and not just identify their errors. The focus on errors is particularly common when teachers mark children's written work and focus inappropriately on the secretarial aspects of the work.

Both oral and written forms of feedback should seek positive outcomes, and include:

- recognition of children's effort and success
- suggestions and questions to support children's development.

Good quality feedback can provide children with a model of the strategies they will need to assess their own work effectively.

Children's self-assessment

So why do children need self-assessment strategies? Clarke (2001) maintains that 'children are less motivated and often demoralised when they are continually compared to each other'(p. 74), and self-assessment can address this problem. It encourages children to become actively involved in their own learning. Hall and Burke (2003) maintain that it also 'empowers learners to take control and assume ownership over their learning and recognise that they themselves are ultimately responsible for their own learning' (p. 53). Once children develop self-assessment strategies, they will be able to set or negotiate targets relevant to their own specific needs.

Reporting to parents

Reporting to parents is a statutory requirement in most English-speaking countries, and usually includes written reports and parent/teacher meetings. Both forms of reporting should:

- provide parents with an honest appraisal of their child's progress and development in all aspect of English
- identify areas of strength and areas for development in speaking and listening, reading and writing, provided in language parents can understand.

In meetings with parents it is possible to show (carefully marked) samples of children's written work.

Writing reports is time-consuming, and many schools now provide teachers with software to support this process. While this is acceptable, reports still need to represent what you have been teaching in English, and give evidence idiosyncratic to each child's development in English.

Conclusion

In this chapter we have examined the practical aspects of teaching a complex and dynamic subject that underpins children's ability to be successful not only as communicators (through oracy and literacy), but also in other areas of the curriculum. With the recognition that learning must be purposeful and enjoyable now formally acknowledged in documents such as *Excellence and Enjoyment* (DfES, 2003) and *Every Child Matters* (DfES, 2004), the creativity of practitioners is now valued and encouraged. With this endorsement the teaching of English can be taught as it should be – excellently, and with enjoyment.

References

Briggs, M., Martin, C., Swatton, P. and Woodfield, A. (2003), *Assessment for Learning and Teaching in Primary Schools: Achieving QTS*. Exeter: Learning Matters.

Browne, A. (2001), *Developing Language and Literacy 3–8* (3rd edition). London: Paul Chapman.

Bruner, J. (1966), *Towards a Theory of Instruction*. Cambridge, Mass: Harvard University Press.

Clarke, S. (2001), *Unlocking Formative Assessment: Practical Strategies for Enhancing Pupils' Learning in the Primary Classroom*. London: Hodder and Stoughton.

Department for Education and Employment (1999), *The Management, Role and Training of Learning Support Assistants*. Centre for Educational Needs: University of Manchester.

Department for Education and Skills (DfES) (2003), *Excellence and Enjoyment: A Strategy for Primary Schools*. London: DfES.

Department for Education and Skills (2004), *Every Child Matters: Change for Children in Schools*. London: DfES.

Hall, K. and Burke, W. (2003), *Making Formative Assessment Work: Effective Practice in the Primary Classroom*. Berkshire: Open University Press.

Headington, R. (2000), *Monitoring, Assessment, Recording, Reporting and Accountability: Meeting the Standards*. London: David Fulton.

Johnston, R.R. (2001), 'What is children's literature?' in G. Winch, R.R. Johnston, P. March, L. Ljungdahl and M. Holliday, *Literacy: Reading, Writing and Children's Literature*. Sydney: Oxford University Press.

Mallett, M. (2002), *The Primary English Encyclopaedia*. London: David Fulton.

Rudd, A. and Tyldesley, A. (2006), *Literacy and ICT in the Primary School*. London: David Fulton.

Teaching English: Beyond the Curriculum

Russell Jones and William Cooper

Introduction

Teacher: What I'd like you to do is build two towers using the unifix.

Harry: Can I build a car?

Teacher: No Harry, I would like two…

Joshua: Look! Look! I've built a castle!

Teacher: No Joshua, I would like a tower. All I want you to do is put the unifix together and make a tower.

Austin: I've done mine, can I go now?

Teacher: Well done Austin. Everyone look at Austin, how sensible! He has built a tower with no fuss.

Kieran: It looks like a snake, I'm going to build a snake.

Teacher: Yes it does look like a snake. Alright, when you have finished I would like you to build another one but not the same size. Harry you haven't started yet.

Harry: I want to build a car. I'm pretendi…

Austin: I've done them both now. Look Miss X I've done them both now, look I've done them both.

Teacher: Okay everyone, look at Austin's two towers.

Kieran: You said we could have snakes!

Teacher: Everyone look at Austin's snakes. I'm going to lie them down on the table and I want you to tell me a word that describes the snakes.

The group sits in silence

Teacher: This snake here is sssss…

Harry: Stupid!

The group all start laughing

Teacher: No, think of a word to describe the snake. Sssss…

Kieran: Small!

Teacher: Well done Kieran, that is an excellent word to describe the snake, but I'm thinking of a different word that is similar to 'small'…

Austin: Sssss…

Teacher: It starts with sh…

Austin: Shirm…erm…

Teacher: Shor…

All together: SHORT!

Teacher: Well done! Now let's look at the other snake. Is this snake bigger or smaller than that one?

Harry: Big!

Teacher: Yes, it is bigger. So if that snake is short then this one is…

Austin: Massive!

Teacher: That isn't the word I'm looking for. It begins with 'L'.

Silence

Teacher: L…L…Lon…

Kieran: Long!

Teacher: Very good. Now what I'd like you all to do is build a long snake and a short snake.

The children begin constructing their snakes

Harry: I've finished mine.

Teacher: Okay Harry, using the two words we have just learned, tell me about your snakes.

Harry: That one is big and that one is small.

Teacher: No Harry, remember what we said, that one is sho…

Harry: That one is big.

Teacher: Can anyone else tell me about their snakes? Go on then Joshua.

Joshua: That one is big and that one is littler.

Teacher: Austin, can you tell me about your snakes?

Austin: That one is short and that one is long.

Teacher: Well done Austin! You have been listening haven't you? Go and ask Miss Y for a sticker. Okay, Kieran can you tell me about your snakes?

Kieran: That one is long and that one is small.

Teacher: Well done everyone. You have worked hard. You can go and choose now and we'll look at this again tomorrow.

So, no problem there then. The teacher achieved her objectives, the children all learned how to use the correct terminology to describe snakes made out of unifix, and now the class can move on to their next learning experience. This transcript was recorded and transcribed by a student teacher watching one of her colleagues at work in an Early Years setting, and was submitted as part of a portfolio of evidence based on a school experience. Of course it provides us with all kinds of starting points to discuss the whole business of interaction between adults and children in educational settings: but, for now, we would like to think about this activity within wider notions of 'creativity'.

What should teachers *do* about creativity?

As adults, we regularly express our admiration for those examples of creativity that we come across in our daily lives: the startling piece of innovative design, the way that a character's development turns unexpectedly in a film and confounds our expectations, the way that a piece of music can sample an apparently random source and turn it into an infectious and unforgettable song. The list is endless, but the point is that we *notice* this, we *value* this and we feel as though this is genuine evidence of creative minds at work.

At the very same time, we seem to live in an educational climate where almost the opposite is the norm. The child who does not meet the teacher's objective for the lesson because she spent too long wondering 'What if this was done in a different way?' has now become a *problem*. What should the teacher *do*? The child who has taken an initial idea in a literacy lesson about writing conversation in the form of a play script has instead created two pages of fascinating exchange between two characters, and none of it has been set out 'correctly', and so the teacher's objectives have clearly not been met. Tomorrow we move on to punctuation in play scripts so there is not time to go back and work with this. What should the teacher *do*?

All too often creativity is seen as a problem. Thinking 'outside the box' in modern education climates and settings creates all kinds of managerial problems for educators; and yet this is actually what we hope children will do once they have the right 'building blocks' in place. Why are we so threatened when children demonstrate the individuality, spontaneity and creativity that we value so highly and hold as aspirational goals in our classrooms? Perhaps the first thing that needs to be said is that teachers need to be creative in order to be effective in their job. We have come through an age of institutional compliance and have emerged at the point where even the inspectorate acknowledges that this is the case:

> Teachers and school leaders have to recognise that the development of creativity in pupils is an essential part of their job, and that an appropriate climate has to be established. (Ofsted, 2003: 11)

This kind of explicit recognition of the value of creative thinking, and support for classroom practitioners who embraced creative approaches, was not always so visible. If we take a step back only four years or so there were virtually no publications on shelves that encouraged beginning teachers to work creatively (and now we have a new wealth of publications to examine). Similarly, the Department for Education and Employment's (DfEE's) first attempts at a website on creativity tied itself in pedagogical knots as it attempted to insist that creativity could only happen as long as the teacher's stated outcomes and objectives were being met. It is more than encouraging to see the huge shift in thinking that has taken place in recent years, and trainees and beginning teachers should feel supported in the choices they make when attempting to establish more creative principles and practices in their classrooms.

Pause to think

When were the moments in your own experience as a child when you felt you were being genuinely creative? Were these moments inside or outside the classroom? Did they arise out of suggestions made by the teacher, or were they the result of questions asked by children? Were these moments prolonged – did they happen over a significant period of time – or were they fleeting? Who else became aware of these moments? Was there an audience for the outcome? Above all: why do you remember these moments as a learner. and how might they influence you as a teacher?

Plan for creativity

Texts for beginning teachers often begin by asking trainees to consider what kinds of classrooms they want. This seems such a simple starting point, and yet it is an incredibly complex beginning, as so many (often competing) dimensions need to be considered. How does my creative lesson meet the school's aims? How is progression ensured if children are not aiming to meet my objectives? How can creativity be assessed? Am I still an effective teacher if my lesson plans are abandoned because a child came up with a more interesting idea? How is it possible to plan for creativity?

Perhaps trainees need a different starting point. Listening to beginning teachers talk about their experiences and their work in school, it can often be the case that they feel they entered their training wanting to effect 'change', and wanting to be highly motivated and highly motivational in their classroom, but gradually feel this is eroded as they learn instead to plan, to control, to assess, to evaluate, to *teach* rather than inspire. We would argue that these are genuine concerns, but that teaching and inspiring are not necessarily mutually exclusive. The rest of this chapter will attempt to grapple with this as a huge philosophical and practical dilemma and, hopefully, to empower beginning teachers in their desire to build the classrooms they want rather than feel their skills are tempered by compliance.

Creativity is not a new feature of the classroom. It has a history of its own. What *is* new is the climate in which creative lessons are expected to exist. At the same time as the curriculum was at its most prescriptive (with the introduction of sequential and highly stylized teaching in mathematics and literacy on top of a highly prescriptive and hierarchical curriculum), the publication of *All Our Futures: Creativity, Culture and Education* suggested that many teachers were attempting to be creative *in spite of* the curriculum rather than because of it (NACCCE, 1999: 8). Similarly, it claimed that there were 'deep concerns about…the extent to which current training takes account of the importance of creative and cultural education' (NACCCE, 1999: 9). It is unsurprising that the current climate has left many beginning teachers feeling as though creativity is something that has to be negotiated or controlled rather than something that genuinely informs the day-to-day business of teaching and learning. A contemporary response to this issue has been identified, and beginning teachers and their trainers have begun to negotiate these problems: but as Craft (2005) points out, this process 'also problematises creativity. It has brought with it exploration of the tensions and dilemmas encapsulated in fostering it' (p. 16).

In many ways, this encapsulates the problem: on the one hand creativity should be part of the culture of the classroom; but on the other hand, beginning teachers have to then discuss the dilemmas they face when trying to be creative while also achieving their stated lesson objectives. In this respect, the Primary Strategy can be seen as merely reaffirming teacher-led notions of creativity in their stated notions of 'good literacy teaching' when:

> The literacy skills and knowledge that children are expected to learn are clearly defined and *the teacher has mapped out how to lead the children to the intended learning* [emphasis added]. (Department for Education and Skills, 2006: 19)

There is evidence, however, that this negotiated process is not only recognized but is beginning to inform the way that beginning teachers are taught:

> Education is now beginning to take account of recent research into the way the brain works and the ways in which children learn and to relate this to the teaching and learning of today's curriculum. The result is likely to be an increase in creative and multi-sensory approaches to teaching, linked to clearly defined learning objectives. (Baldwin and Fleming, 2004: 4)

A distinction has been made between 'soft' creativity, which typically may include arts-based teaching characterized by 'colourful, rather manic, activity', and psychology-focused creativity, where 'a sudden moment of abrupt illumination, in which the solution to a previously intractable problem leaps into consciousness fully formed, without any immediately preceding process of methodical, rational problem-solving' (Claxton, 2006: 352). While these polar positions may seem stereotypical and simplistic, there are lessons here for classroom teachers. Just as 'creativity' is not about blinding flashes of genius where the greater mysteries of the world suddenly reveal themselves in all their wonder and complexity, so neither is 'creativity' gummed paper squares on a Friday afternoon once all the 'real' work of the week has been successfully negotiated.

Perhaps we need to characterize creativity rather than define it, and in so doing this may resonate more closely with beginning teachers' perceptions of creative work in the classroom.

Encourage genuinely open-ended inquiry

If the teacher already knows the outcome, then there is not much point in pretending that creativity is taking place. Children may eventually locate the outcome through their own endeavours, but if all they are doing is confirming the teacher's expectations then we need to ask questions about how far any of this is genuinely creative. Think about the interaction with the unifix at the start of this chapter. How far were the children able to explore the materials without stepping outside the teacher's pre-determined boundaries?

Show (and appreciate the value of) the seams

In the same example, the real value of the activity lies in the creative responses demonstrated by the children. Their developing imagination and creative use of vocabulary is continually harnessed and brought back to the objectives of the activity by the teacher. How much more valuable might it have been to abandon the initial objective and instead explore the different responses to the same activity and use the children's enthusiasm and imagination as an opportunity to carry out some really supportive language work?

Resist the teacher's pre-formed notions of 'correctness'

In the unifix transcript, it is only too obvious that 'correctness' is the purpose of the exercise. The children cannot be 'right' unless they finally arrive at the teacher's version of 'correctness'. Notions of 'short' and 'long' in this exercise could have been strengthened considerably by *listening* to the children's responses instead of guiding them towards mouthing the only two words that counted in the exercise.

Think carefully about ownership of the project

If a project is to be considered genuinely 'creative' then ownership of the process is paramount. A teacher may well have set up an interesting problem or initiated a particular line of inquiry; but if the teacher is looking for creative responses to the project then the child needs to demonstrate a decision-making process in action. Resources, collaboration with peers, access to further information, time limits and final outcomes are all part of that decision-making process, and are all elements that children can bring to the task in a creative context.

How is creativity 'measured' in a classroom context?

Children need to be secure in the knowledge that their creative responses will not be dissected and probed unrelentingly until all sense of interest or potential has been cleansed from the project. If they have been encouraged to work 'without a safety-net', if they have been told that they have the space to test some of their own ideas, then there is little point in expecting a finished, polished outcome 15 minutes later. If teachers are to measure and discuss creative outcomes then they need to feel comfortable talking more about ideas, potential and possibilities than concrete outcomes.

Teachers and parents often marvel at the way young children interact with technology. They admire the way that something so complex and challenging in an adult world can seem so intuitive and natural for children. They often watch in awe as children decide what they need to do and then test out a series of hypotheses in order to locate their way forward, and then polish and shape this process through a decision-making process that is bold, questioning, confident and unafraid. These same adults then ask why children's writing is so formulaic, dull or uninspired, seeing no connection between the two observations.

Children's work in literacy (for example) is not going to be genuinely creative if it is continually held up for public scrutiny and criticism. They are not likely to 'test the water' by using challenging vocabularies when they are likely to be penalized for their spelling. When children explore technology, they do so with the knowledge that their mistakes are private; when children explore literacy, their mistakes can be public and painful.

Rather than teachers looking to identify creative pupils, or creative components to their lesson planning, we suggest that there would be more value instead in thinking about creative communities or creative classrooms. In thinking this way, teachers and learners are part of the same dynamic process: both are seeking individual, original and imaginative responses within an appreciative and encouraging environment. Just as teachers would like to see children move away from the predictable line of thought in order to test a more creative response, so do children need to see teachers step outside their lesson planning to demonstrate respect and appreciation when that happens. If these two approaches happen as part of a creative classroom culture then there are likely to be more genuinely creative moments.

What does creativity in the classroom *look* like?

Let us continue by saying that creativity is desirable in the classroom. It is valuable, it is aspirational, it is *necessary* in the effective classroom. School effectiveness cannot be measured accurately if teaching and learning is a mechanical process that does not support creative relationships and approaches in primary classrooms. The classroom that is dominated by the teacher can never be truly effective as a genuine teaching and learning environment, because the learning and teaching that takes place is already defined, shaped and controlled by the process of working to meet clearly stated lesson objectives that are copied studiously from the National Curriculum or the Primary Strategy.

Let us take an extreme example: a part of a literacy lesson where a group of children are 'working independently' on a piece of writing. It is an all-too-familiar scenario to imagine: the teacher reminds the group what the objectives are for this piece of writing, she has decided which children are working together, she decides how long there is before the task is completed, she decided which tools and resources are available to complete the task, she decides who the audience will be once it is completed, she decides whether the children are allowed to talk about their work or write in silence, and as a passing afterthought on her way to working with her focus group she reminds them to 'try to be really creative'.

Of course, this is an issue of power in the classroom, and the problem with the above scenario is the word 'decide'. It is here that many beginning teachers can find their practical entry point into more creative classrooms. If the teacher is the one who 'decides' everything that happens, when it happens, how it relates to the next thing that happens etc. etc., then creativity is always going to be a problem. If, conversely, children are encouraged to make real decisions about their experiences as learners then creativity can be nurtured and can flourish. It begins with a simple step: have the confidence to believe that children are stakeholders in the classroom and that they have valid views as learners. If they are allowed to express these ideas rather than just comply with the teacher's stated lesson objectives then we may have begun to establish a different kind of climate for the classroom:

> ...the successful lessons...were ones where current prescribed practice was overturned. The most creative lessons were ones where there was a different kind of relationship in the classroom, one that was not about an authoritative figure who held answers, resources and power, but one which was based on mutual respect, trust and, above all, enquiry. These class-

rooms asked questions of themselves. Pupils were not afraid to ask the question 'Wouldn't it be more interesting if we did it this way?', and teachers were not afraid to work with these suggestions. In the environments where creativity flourished, it was not because the teachers had carefully organised a creative slot in the term's curriculum; it was because creative approaches and possibilities underpinned the relationship between teachers and learners and the culture of the classroom. (Jones and Wyse, 2004: 4)

Case study

It may be worth looking at the experiences of one university tutor visiting a beginning teacher in a Year 6 setting. What follows is an account offered by the tutor of her observations of learning and teaching in the classroom:

Children in this class were looking at Tudor Britain and had spent some initial time collecting together ideas, key words and phrases, finding out about central characters from the period and so on. At this point, much of the work had been typical and although the children had collected different source material, the process had been the same for everyone.

In subsequent discussions, the children decided that they wanted to find out more about Sir Francis Drake and about what life had really been like on the Golden Hind. Through individual and group research, the children began to piece together a list of skills required for a successful crew. A trades committee was appointed and children had to apply for jobs on the 'ship'. Parents were invited into the school to contribute, and a loose 'script' was written by several of the children relating to events that might have been encountered on the Golden Hind. Children in role were encouraged to use vocabulary relevant to their assumed trade. Tudor music provided the background for the role play.

Once this process had been concluded, the teacher asked the children to reflect on their feelings. How had the drama developed their knowledge of life as a seafarer? How important was their trade to the overall success of the voyage? How did their character relate to other characters? Most importantly from a historical perspective, the children were asked to think about the importance of the various roles, and whose historical versions of the events were actually known to later generations. In achieving this, it became clear that pupils had needed to synthesize their known information with a sense of imagined empathy in order to create a closer understanding of what the voyage might have genuinely been like for the ship's crew.

Whereas the teacher had created a creative climate in the classroom, the children had initiated the real process of making meaning within this context. The teacher, as a facilitator of learning, clearly knew when to prompt, when to push and when to tease responses from individuals; the pupils, rather than mirror a previously determined outcome, became genuinely

> ### Case study (continued)
>
> active in the way that they used their developing sense of empathy, their collected sources of information and their collaborative and purposeful talk to gain a closer understanding of human experience that later informed a dramatic performance. This is, of course, in complete contrast to the 'unifix' transcript offered at the start of this chapter.

The above case study is an example of 'process drama' as opposed to 'performance drama'. Whereas performance drama puts the audience at the centre of the activity, O'Neill (1995) argues that process drama is child-centred. Rather than focus on the performance as an outcome, it is argued that *the whole experience* is for the benefit of the child, the richness lying in the process itself, and valuing the quality of the associated talk and the development of imagined worlds just as much as any performance-related outcome:

> When we read, we draw on our own experiences of life and other stories to make our individual meanings. With drama activities, children are able to enter the world of the texts to examine the ambiguities and uncertainties from the inside and, within the classroom, to experience literary meaning-making communities…the social and active experience of learning comes to the fore through drama work of this nature. (Lambirth, 2005: 86–7).

This point of view has been considerably reinforced recently, and has seen a growing call from politicians and influential educationalists for teachers in all sectors of the state system to be more creative and innovative in their teaching styles.

In the current multi-professional climate, it is not incidental that the Sure Start website reminds all child-focused professionals that:

> Creativity is part of every area of the curriculum and all areas of learning have the potential to be creative experiences. The creative process, which includes curiosity, exploration, play and creativity, is as applicable to Personal, Social and Emotional Development; Communication, Language and Literacy; Mathematical Development; Knowledge and Understanding of the World and Physical Development as it is to art, music, dance and imaginative play. (Duffy, 2004: 6)

The current status of creativity in the curriculum

Having already identified a possible mood swing in the 3–11 curriculum, it is important that mention is made of the focus and stance in the recently published Primary National Strategy. Supporters of the National Literacy Strategy argue that the shared and guided reading approaches advocated in that document promoted creative thinking and discussion, and that by 'responding imaginatively' as required by the National Curriculum's references to group discussions an environment should already exist to foster creativity. Others might disagree.

There is no doubt however, that the publication of *Excellence and Enjoyment* (DfES, 2003) has required teachers to include more active and personal learning within literacy lessons, and teachers have been encouraged to anticipate and encourage creative and personal responses in their pupils. This can be a challenge for those teachers who feel insecure in the area of literacy, but children will rise to meet these expectations. When children move outside mechanical responses to set tasks and realize that their literacy 'voices' have value, it is our experience that the resulting sense of motivation can be exhilarating.

The supporters of creative approaches to education are likely to welcome the central role of speaking and listening in the Primary National Strategy, which includes a discrete drama strand in the new literacy strategy, alongside the statement that 'the revisions emphasise the importance of reading independently and reading for pleasure'(DfES, 2006: 15). While there is evidence here that creativity is to be encouraged and valued, teachers need to remember that it is not children who need to be told the value of creativity. Children use words creatively in their storytelling and in their imaginative play. They own the stories and fictions they create and are naturally motivated to share them with their peers. When looked at in this way, play leading to drama is essential in order for all children to practise their language development and to contribute to the learning process.

This is one creative approach that enhances the children's learning experience in developing reading skills and strategies. The challenge for teachers is to extend their repertoire in order to accommodate the visual, auditory and kinaesthetic preferred learning styles of the children in their class across the curriculum areas. Imperative to this creative approach is the need for teachers to reflect upon their role in providing a supportive classroom ethos that values the learners' input. Kendall-Seatter comments:

> There seems to be an over-emphasis on the teacher having a clear idea of his/her own working requirements...how to get the children to behave as the teacher wants rather than being a negotiation about how all involved are going to work in the shared learning space. (Kendall-Seatter, 2005: 91)

Conclusion

So, what does 'creativity' really *mean* for beginning teachers? It is helpful to think of creativity not as a 'blueprint' for the classroom but as the accumulated result, over time, of classroom contexts and cultures that encourage and support risk-taking. This is not easy for new teachers to adopt, and it takes considerable courage for even experienced teachers to embrace: but we would argue that it is in the interests of children and teachers alike to promote this kind of interaction.

Creative 'success' cannot be measured in traditional forms, and if teachers set out to measure creativity against level descriptors they will fail. Creative success comes over time, as confidence, trust and opportunities evolve. As teachers learn that sometimes (often!) children have ideas that are stronger than the teacher, so children will learn that they work in a climate where their suggestions, ideas, hypotheses and imaginings are all valued as integral to their learning experience.

References

Baldwin, P. and Fleming, K. (2004), *Teaching Literacy Through Drama*. London: Routledge Falmer.

Claxton, G. (2006), 'Thinking at the edge.' *Cambridge Journal of Education* 36 (3), September, 351–62.

Craft, A. (2005), 'Changes in the landscape for creativity in education' in A. Wilson (ed), *Creativity in Primary Education*. Exeter: Learning Matters.

Department for Education and Skills (2003), *Excellence and Enjoyment: A Strategy for Primary Schools*. London: DfES.

Department for Education and Skills (2006), *Primary National Strategy: Primary Framework for Literacy and Mathematics*. London: DfES.

Duffy, B. (2004), *Supporting Creativity and Imagination in the Early Years* (2nd edition). Maidenhead: Open University.

Jones, R. and Wyse, D. (2004), *Creativity in the Primary Curriculum*. London: David Fulton.

Kendall-Seatter, S. (2005), *Reflective Reader: Primary Professional Studies*. Exeter: Learning Matters.

Lambirth, A. (2005), *Reflective Reader: Primary English*. Exeter: Learning Matters.

National Advisory Committee on Creative and Cultural Education (1999), *All Our Futures: Creativity, Culture and Education*. Sudbury: DfEE.

Ofsted (2003), *Expecting the Unexpected*. www.ofsted.gov.uk/publications

O'Neill, C. (1995), *Drama Worlds: A Framework for Process Drama*. Portsmouth: Heinemann.

Teaching Mathematics: The Principles

Ian Sugarman

Chapter Outline

We used to think that if we knew one, we knew two, because one and one are two. We are finding that we must learn a great deal more about 'and'.

Sir Arthur Eddington (1882–1944) in Mackay (1977)

Introduction

In this chapter we will consider the place of mathematics in the school curriculum and ask the question: What does it mean to learn mathematics? Skemp's distinction between 'instrumental' and 'relational' understanding is discussed, as are links between this and constructivist theories of learning. Understanding errors and recognizing and anticipating misconceptions about mathematical ideas is seen as essential knowledge for a teacher of mathematics. The National Numeracy Strategy of England and Wales is seen as a major influence on the teaching of mathematics, and we examine the problematic nature of one of its central concerns: interactive teaching. Using and applying mathematics is also raised as a major issue that teachers need to address.

The place of mathematics in the curriculum

Mathematics has enjoyed such a long established position on the school curriculum that it might seem curious to ask this question at all. But when we remind ourselves that the real reason it was included in the first place was so that there should be sufficient numbers of people trained in the written arithmetical routines to be able to undertake bookkeeping and accounting procedures in a standardized manner, we can begin to understand some of the current issues to do with teaching methodology.

That priority has long since disappeared, and the teaching of mathematics, in its wider sense, has for many decades been seen as part of a wider objective of having a population both literate and numerate as educationally desirable in its own right. The preamble to the Mathematics National Curriculum (DfEE, 1999) provides a rationale for the subject's inclusion in the school curriculum:

> Mathematics equips pupils with a uniquely powerful set of tools to understand and change the world. These tools include logical reasoning, problem-solving skills, and the ability to think in abstract ways.
>
> Mathematics is important in everyday life, many forms of employment, science and technology, medicine, the economy, the environment and development, and in public decision-making.
>
> Different cultures have contributed to the development and application of mathematics. Today, the subject transcends cultural boundaries and its importance is universally recognised.
>
> Mathematics is a creative discipline. It can stimulate moments of pleasure and wonder when a pupil solves a problem for the first time, discovers a more elegant solution to that problem, or suddenly sees hidden connections. (p. 60)

Here, there is a bold and clear recognition that there is more to mathematics than the knowledge of some basic calculating procedures. Whereas the first two paragraphs refer to the diverse uses to which mathematical knowledge can be put, the final one indicates that it has much to offer as a special way of thinking that is accessible to all, and not just to an elite of mathematical boffins.

What is mathematics?

One often hears people describing themselves or others as 'not good at maths'. While there may be some meaning conveyed by this expression on a conversational level, it can conceal more than it reveals. Which aspects of mathematics are being referred to? It might refer to some generalized weakness in working with numbers, or even anxiety produced at the thought of having to think through a number problem, or it might be a deficiency in one or more of these particular skills:

- remembering the meaning of *terms* such as 'factor' or 'product', or *notation* such as '3^2'
- remembering number *facts* such as multiplication tables or number bonds (e.g. what goes with 4 to make 10)

- understanding the meaning of some kinds of numbers (e.g. fractions or negative numbers)
- remembering how to carry out some kinds of *written calculations* (e.g. subtraction by decomposition)
- awareness of *strategies* that draw on recalled facts to derive ones that are not recalled (e.g. use 6+6=12 to work out 7+6)
- understanding *relationships between operations* to enable calculations to be undertaken mentally (e.g. use addition facts to derive subtractions)
- understanding how mathematical concepts interrelate (e.g. fractions, decimals and percentages).

Given the wide range of meanings 'maths' can have, it is essential that teachers are clear about the nature of the competences with which they are dealing. We would regard this version of 'subject knowledge' as even more crucial for primary teachers than the ability to solve questions posed in a GCSE mathematics paper learned in a rote fashion. Learning mathematics can be a problematic endeavour, and being able to identify the different elements of 'the territory' is surely a precondition for a teacher of mathematics being effective.

Although published in 1985, *Mathematics from 5 to 16* still provides an extremely useful delineation of the components of the mathematics curriculum. It enumerates:

A. Facts (four objectives)
B. Skills (five objectives)
C. Conceptual structures (five objectives)
D. General strategies (eight objectives)
E. Personal qualities (two objectives)

While no-one would dispute the responsibility of the teacher in helping pupils learn those objectives in A to D (the content of the mathematics curriculum, much of which has remained virtually unchanged for many decades), the objectives to do with pupils' work habits, such as being systematic, imaginative, persevering, and those to do with having a positive attitude to the subject, are also the responsibility of the teacher. Indeed, children's negative attitudes towards mathematics are invariably due to their teacher's refusal to take that responsibility on board.

Providers of school mathematics syllabuses, including the National Curriculum of England and Wales, slice up the content into similar headings, usually into Number, Shape and Space, Measures and Handling Data. Each of these is subdivided again. The National Numeracy Strategy for England and Wales (now Primary National Strategy) has gone one stage further and specified a teaching programme based around the teaching of specific learning objectives.

Given the wide-ranging content of the mathematics syllabus, it falls upon any teaching programme to outline how that content can be delivered. What the Primary National Strategy has done is to identify a very large number of discrete learning objectives and cluster these as units of work that last about two to three weeks. Although a non-statutory document, it provides a model for how these learning objectives might be covered during the course of the year for each age group, from Reception to Year 6. Most schools in England prefer to use either this model or a commercial scheme that is based upon it.

What to teach?

Much of what is currently the subject of debate in the world of mathematics education concerns questions of how to teach in the classroom (such as teaching styles). However, there are signs that there is an undeclared assumption that the correct way to teach the long list of learning objectives is to make each one a lesson focus. When the Department for Education and Skills (DfES) made available sets of model lesson plans (see references list), it distributed the learning objectives on an almost one-to-one basis. Clearly, lessons do need to have a focus. But, instead of that focus isolating a discrete area of mathematical knowledge it could aim to locate concepts within a *context*, with a view to identifying and highlighting the ways in which they interrelate. Mathematics is essentially a coherent network of interrelated ideas and skills, and the logic of this network can be obscured if concepts and skills are taught in a piecemeal fashion. An alternative approach is for pupils to be asked to investigate an interesting situation or try to solve a problem, and in so doing, to engage with the nature and limits of their mathematical knowledge. The teacher's role is then to identify common issues that arise, which might be the focus for follow-up lessons of the other type. What the teacher is doing is discovering the *need* for a lesson with a particular focus, rather than presuming it.

This sensible principle is present in the model (Figure 4.1) the Numeracy Strategy would like teachers to adopt when planning a unit of work lasting two to three weeks.

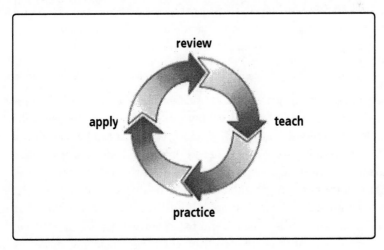

Figure 4.1 The review/teach/practice/apply model

A reviewing exercise is seen as both the first and last stage of the cycle. The Numeracy Strategy's advice is to:

> Review children's previous learning in an introductory lesson, possibly a problem-solving lesson in which children can demonstrate what they know and can do. (DfES, 2006)

However, there are at least two problematic issues contained within this guidance. The first is to do with what is meant by 'a problem-solving lesson'. As will be seen later in this chapter, the way in which problem solving, as part of using and applying mathematics, is incorporated into the mathematics curriculum is a central issue in mathematics education. Pupils do not readily transfer their knowledge to contextualized problems when it has been taught in a context-free, 'pure' mathematical situation. There is a substantial risk therefore that teachers can misinterpret the causes of failure of a task when it is presented as a problem, as there are so many potential reasons.

- Have pupils misunderstood the meaning of the problem?
- Have they understood the problem but failed to identify an appropriate mathematical strategy?
- Have they identified an appropriate strategy but made an arithmetical error in applying it?
- Was a mathematical error merely a lapse of concentration or the result of a misconception?

Naturally, each of these would need to be addressed in a different way. The Primary Strategy's guidance on this matter is as follows:

> Plan questions that will help you to determine whether there are groups of children who need more support before they move on. Identify any children who might benefit from additional challenge as they already have a good understanding of aspects of the work covered in the unit and are already meeting many of the unit's learning objectives or are close to doing so. (DfES, 2006)

A formidable challenge for teachers is to translate the evidence they obtain from their class of around 30 pupils into an effective teaching strategy, determining what will be appropriate learning objectives for which groups of children, and what can be relevantly addressed with the whole class. In doing so, they will need to balance those concerns to do with effective pupils' learning and those to do with manageability of the whole class.

These issues are being highlighted early on in this section, not in order to frighten or daunt you into the seeming impossibility of the scale of the task, but to signal the importance of needing to be realistic, and to acknowledge at an early stage that 'getting it right' for every single pupil is not a realistic enterprise. Teaching strategies that promote independent thinking, collaborative working and exploit the interrelated nature of mathematical ideas will do more to ameliorate the complexities of trying to determine the learning outcomes of every single pupil in the class than efforts to individualize the teaching experience of each student.

What is 'understanding'?

Earlier in the chapter, when identifying some of the possible weaknesses in being able to 'do maths', there was frequent use of the word 'understanding' alongside 'remembering'. One often hears adults referring to a computational skill that they have remembered learning at school, like how to multiply fractions, while having little idea why this procedure works. This is sometimes referred to as a distinction between knowing *what* to do but without knowing *why*. Skemp (1991) characterizes this as the difference between 'instrumental understanding' and 'relational understanding'.

He uses the analogy of coping with finding your way around an unfamiliar town. Instrumental understanding would involve the memorizing of a set of instructions to get you from one particular place to another; whereas relational understanding is gained from exploring the town to get an overall mental map of it. His argument is that this latter form of understanding is much more beneficial, because it equips you with the means to solve a range of problems, including how to cope with getting lost.

Elsewhere, Skemp (1972) contrasts 'habit learning' and 'intelligent learning' as:

> ...two different kinds of learner-teacher relationship and two states of mind. Habit learning keeps the learner dependent on being told what to do in every new situation, with little confidence in his own ability to cope if left on his own. Intelligent learning develops the learner's confidence in his own ability to deal with any situation which can be understood in relation to his existing knowledge, and encourages perception of the teacher as someone who can help him to increase this knowledge, and thereby his power of understanding.
> (pp. 44–5)

The challenge for trainee and newly qualified primary teachers is to avoid teaching mathematics 'instrumentally', by seeking objectives that are easily translatable into routines that rely heavily upon memory for their execution. Instead, the aim should be to find ways of engaging pupils in gaining a feel for the 'territory' they are working in, with a view to them appreciating a rationale for the skills and routines that are available. This approach is particularly fertile ground for allowing pupils to generate their own, invented strategies. Very often, these seemingly idiosyncratic solutions turn out to be simply reformulations of existing known ones. But the important point here is that strategies that have been invented by pupils can easily be re-invented by them through a process of meaning-making. This is totally different from having to learn them rote-fashion, where there is a dependence upon the least reliable of our faculties – memory.

A theoretical framework for the teaching of mathematics

Learning through a Constructivist approach

Throughout the twentieth century, successive reports by the Inspectorate on the teaching of mathematics in England and Wales referred to the need for pupils to understand what they are learning about as opposed to simply performing skills in a rote fashion. While the chief purpose of teaching mathematics was considered to be the transmission of standardized arithmetical routines, it could be argued that the most efficient teaching approach was demonstration and practice; but the broadening of the scope of the subject has led to a consideration of the merits of alternative teaching styles.

Constructivist approaches to learning focus more on the relationship between the teacher and the learner within a classroom setting. It regards as problematic the ways in which pupils come to develop meaning, whereas the traditional or exposition role of the teacher sees this as non-problematic. It views the learner as someone who has to actively construct meaning for themselves, in order for a new idea to make sense. One way of characterizing this is as a process of *mathematizing*. Although this is in some respects quite distinct from the content of the mathematics curriculum, the relationship is not mutually exclusive:

> ...mathematising should not be dismissed as simply process. Mathematising *is* content. As children learn to recognize, be intrigued by, and explore patterns, as they begin to overlay and interpret experiences, contexts, and phenomena with mathematical questions, tools (tables and charts), and models, they are constructing an understanding of what it really means to be a mathematician – to organize and interpret their world through a mathematical lens. This is the essence of mathematics. (Fosnot and Dolk, 2001: 9)

It should be possible to see now clear lines of correspondence between a Constructivist approach to developing pupils' learning, and the aim of developing relational understanding.

Discovering misconceptions

Much current thinking about children's learning can be traced back to the theories of Piaget, and in particular his claims that children's intellectual development follows a course that is pre-determined in a biological sense. More recently, attention has been focused on the classroom context, and the patterns of interaction between the teacher and pupils, and between pupils. However, despite the common association that Piaget has with individualized explanations of how learning takes place, he points out that coping with conflicting ideas is an important stimulus for learning, which therefore benefits from discussion. This is important, since many teachers might consider it their primary responsibility as being to prevent pupils from making mistakes.

There do appear to be remarkable similarities in the kinds of errors that children make when learning mathematics. This means that teachers with a knowledge of these typical errors are able to anticipate the difficulties encountered by their pupils. In Chapter 5 we will see that setting up situations designed to elicit pupils' misconceptions and then to confront them is a valuable teaching strategy.

Piaget (1970) describes learning as a dual process of *assimilating* new ideas within an existing framework as well as having to alter that framework to *accommodate* new cases that challenge it. An example of this is children's introduction to subtraction as essentially a process of 'taking something away'. They learn that, regardless of the quantity being removed, the easiest way to discover how many remain is to enact a counting strategy to remove a quantity from the total. At a later stage, they learn that with some subtractions, especially those where the number to be subtracted is very close to the original total, it is less cumbersome to count (or add) on from the larger to the smaller number. But this new procedure does not invalidate the earlier model – it can exist alongside it, or be *assimilated*.

However, in the process of learning how to subtract, when the objects are not available for touching or physically removing, there is a need to keep track of the counting by symbolizing the objects, often by using fingers. What some children mistakenly do is to count on from the number that is to be removed ('subtrahend'), but making that the first number in the count. The Figure 4.2 shows this happening when attempting to solve 11 – 8. The child counts from eight and includes this finger in the count. The finger identified as 'eleven' then yields the answer 'four'. Figure 4.3 shows a correct use of finger-counting to solve the problem.

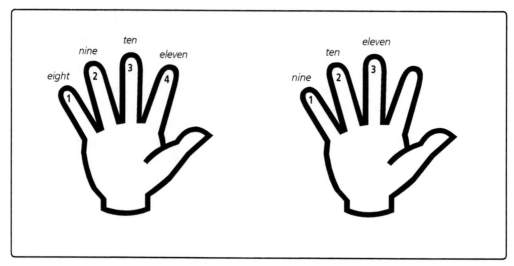

Figure 4.2 An incorrect use of finger counting to solve 11– 8

Figure 4.3 A correct use of finger counting to solve 11– 8

When teachers know that this is a common misconception, they can pay particular attention to how their pupils are enacting the counting process and, if necessary, draw their attention to the two alternatives. Discussing both actions is more likely to lead to an increased awareness of which makes more sense and to decrease the chance that pupils adopt an *instrumental* response – that is, doing what they think they have been told to do without understanding why.

One way of alerting children to this error is to model the process of subtraction on a number track. In Figure 4.4, the eight spaces (representing the eight objects to be subtracted) are highlighted, perhaps by shading them in or by crossing them out. This reveals that to count the remaining numbers you start counting *after* the eight, by saying nine, ten, eleven.

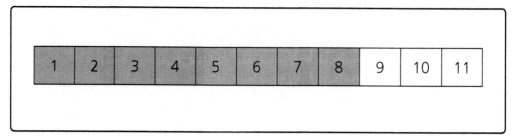

Figure 4.4 Number tracking

Why the need for a national strategy?

Many trainees who themselves went through English primary schools in the 1970s, 1980s and 1990s may well have memories of maths lessons as involving ploughing through a textbook on their own. Teachers responded to difficulties on an individualized basis, and the remediation offered tended to be hurried and brief, designed to lead pupils to the answer by the shortest possible route. Maths lessons tended to be unlike other lessons.

The popularity of commercial mathematics schemes rested partly upon the prevailing notion that, given the strongly sequential and hierarchical nature of the subject, children are best left to progress 'at their own rate' rather than as a class, and partly on account of the fact that mathematics is a curriculum area that many primary teachers have regarded as problematic. It is important not to underestimate the attractiveness of the published schemes to teachers, but it is even more important to recognize the pitfalls of reliance upon them. This will be dealt with more fully in Chapter 5.

Concerns about the levels of attainment of English primary school pupils in mathematics have been expressed on a regular basis over a long period of time. The publication of statistical data by TIMSS (Trends in Mathematics and Science Study) in 1995 and 1999 (IEA, 2000) indicated that a wide gap separated English 9 year olds from those in the Pacific Rim countries, as well as some European countries (Netherlands and Belgium).

In explaining the rationale for the National Numeracy Project (the precursor to the National Numeracy Strategy), Straker (1999), later to become Director of the National Numeracy Strategy, cites HMI and OFSTED reports, as confirming the need to remove the pervasive influence of the commercial schemes which 'reduced the teacher to a classroom manager who involved the children in little direct teaching or discussion about their mathematics'. Whereas English schoolchildren tended to be taught from the textbook with low levels of teacher exposition, mathematics lessons in the higher attaining countries were typified by high levels of direct whole class teaching.

Establishing a clear link between mode of teaching and classroom organization and pupil attainment is a complex matter, as the variables are difficult to define precisely. However, Croll (1996) reported only a small degree of correlation between whole-class teaching and pupils' progress, whereas Askew et al (2004) found that whole class and group teaching was a feature of those teachers classified as most effective as well as those classified as less effective.

Another significant contrast between the English primary mathematics curriculum and that of the higher attaining countries was the priority given to the development of mental calculation skills. The commercial mathematics schemes in use in English schools paid little attention to developing oral and mental skills, tending to concentrate much more on the performance of written routines. These concerns were addressed in the Framework of the National Numeracy Strategy (DfEE, 1999b), and renewed in the revised Framework (DfES, 2006).

The four principles of the National Numeracy Strategy

1 Lessons devoted exclusively to mathematics, every day

There had been a fashion in many primary schools to work 'an integrated day' where, at any one time, groups of pupils would be working on different areas of the curriculum. This could be a nightmare of organization for the teacher, and was certainly not an efficient way of deploying his or her time. There also tended to be a very uneven amount of time devoted to the subject across and even within schools.

2 Direct teaching and interactive oral work with the whole class and groups

This principle was intended to counteract the individualization of learning which characterized the use of commercial schemes. The key aspect here is the interactivity that should be a hallmark of lessons, rather than a one-way process with the teacher doing the bulk of the talking and the pupils merely providing the occasional answer to a question.

3 An emphasis upon mental calculation

Underpinning this principle is the aim of getting all pupils to consider whether the calculation in front of them can be done mentally, without recourse to a specific written routine. The ability to do this depends upon the intelligent application of a selected strategy, from a repertoire of alternatives, to fit the actual numbers involved. Efficient mental calculation therefore depends upon a feeling for number, whereas efficient written calculation often relies heavily upon the memorization of a few, specific, 'one-fits-all' procedures.

4 Controlled differentiation

Many schools organize pupils of the same age into sets so that they are with others of a similar level of attainment. However, recent research (Askew et al, 2004) seems to suggest that such an arrangement does not necessarily lead to the gains in pupils' attainment that are often assumed by those schools that opt for it. In fact, it may even slow the progress of lower attaining pupils.

Another rationale used is that this organizational strategy makes it easier for teachers to manage the demands of teaching children at very different levels of attainment. This is especially critical given the aim of teaching the whole class at the same time. Where classes are not set in this way, the advice is to cater for the needs of the range of attainment by preparing work at up to three different levels. There are many ways that a teacher can deal effectively with a class of children at differing levels of attainment, and differentiating the work they do independently is just one of them. In the Netherlands, there is a strong preference for keeping pupils together by providing problems that allow a differentiated level of response.

Principles of good practice

What is 'interactive' teaching?

While it has been possible since the inception of the Numeracy Strategy to point to significant gains in the attainments of pupils taking the standardized tests (SATs) at ages 7 and 11, it is less clear cut as to the reasons for this. Kyriacou and Goulding (2004) reported that 'the overall enhanced gains in pupil competence may in large measure be a reflection of a closer match between what is being taught and what is being tested, rather than greater pupil gains in their understanding of mathematics' (p. 40).

As for the strong promotion of interactive whole class teaching on the part of the National Numeracy Strategy, Askew et al (2004) failed to find examples of teachers tackling calculation in strategic ways as opposed to the traditional approach of demonstration and practice. In other words, whatever changes have taken place in mathematics lessons, there does not appear to be evidence that teachers have adopted an interactive approach in the sense of searching, higher-order questions that seek to challenge and extend pupils' thinking and encourage a greater power to generalize.

However, it is entirely possible to interpret the expression 'interactive teaching' differently. For many teachers, interactivity is all about finding ways of involving pupils in the lesson. Pupils are drawn to the front of the class to help with the use of structured equipment, to write on the board and to operate procedures on some mathematics software activity. In this respect, teachers can secure the attention of the class and engage them in an active way. There is much anecdotal and impressionistic evidence that there has been a significant move in this direction.

But interactive teaching that has aspirations that go beyond the issue of pupils' physical engagement will continue to be a major area of development for new teachers and experienced teachers alike. The challenge is for teachers to exercise their knowledge of the subject in ways that ensure that pupils are solving problems which provoke them into thinking mathematically, rather than simply following instructions.

Using and applying mathematics

We have already stated that the mathematics curriculum of the early twenty-first century resembles that of half a century before it. A growing emphasis has been placed, however, on the ability of pupils to use and apply their mathematical knowledge. This refers to the way in which pupils are able to use their mathematical knowledge in contexts other than purely mathematical ones. This is sometimes known as 'maths across the curriculum', which we will address in Chapter 6: but there are also issues to do with the way in which we introduce pupils to those mathematical ideas themselves, which we will return to in Chapter 5.

Another aspect of this area concerns the ability to think in mathematical ways and to engage in a wide range of behaviours that are typical of the way mathematicians operate. These are broadly concerned with what are sometimes referred to as 'thinking skills', such as using reasoning and logic to determine a sensible course of action, and also encompass a wide range of communication skills to describe and explain how a solution was arrived at.

Pause to think

3			4
			2
	1		
2		4	

This simplified Sudoku puzzle involves the insertion of numbers according to the rule: place the numbers one to four in each row, column and box. It is solved through reasoning, but without arithmetical calculations.

Attached to its section on 'Number at Key Stage Two', the National Curriculum (DfEE, 1999a) contains these teaching requirements:

Pupils should be taught to:

1a make connections in mathematics and appreciate the need to use numerical skills and knowledge when solving problems in other parts of the curriculum

1b break down a more complex problem or calculation into simpler steps before attempting a solution; identify the information needed to carry out the tasks

1d find different ways of approaching a problem to overcome difficulties

1f organise work and refine ways of recording

1i communicate mathematically, using precise mathematical language

1j understand and investigate general statements

1k search for pattern in their results; develop logical thinking and explain their reasoning.

Since the publication of the first National Curriculum in 1988, these objectives have been associated with 'using and applying' mathematics, and are distinct from the specific arithmetical skills and knowledge listed alongside it.

There has been a long held perception among mathematics educationists and enthusiasts (frequently expressed in *Mathematics Teaching* and other journals) that enjoyment of the subject is compromised by excessive use of written exercises which have no apparent purpose other than the practice of a skill. It is sometimes alleged that problem solving was effectively marginalized in the structure of the Framework of the Numeracy Strategy by assigning it a periodic place in the year's schedule of topics. Pupils cannot develop the range of skills outlined above if they are not given opportunities to work on longer or more challenging tasks.

Alternatively, problem solving and investigative work can be viewed as a vital *approach* in the teaching of the subject on a daily basis, rather than as an isolated 'event': it is what pupils do when a teacher engages them in thinking about the mathematics inherent in situations. Given that it is entirely possible to plan lessons without catering for the need to exercise mathematical thinking processes, a hallmark of good mathematics teaching is the ability to ensure that pupils need to reason and explain their reasoning on a regular basis. Sometimes this will be through working on a problem or puzzle activity, and sometimes simply by inviting a pupil to explain to others why they think their answer is correct.

Conclusion

Many people have developed a negative attitude towards mathematics. In large part, this is a response to the way in which the subject was taught to them at school. Some explain their dislike because of the lack of relevance many of the skills have to their daily lives (although this tends to pertain more to secondary rather than primary school mathematics). Embedding mathematics in real situations is an enterprise that many children appreciate, especially when the work centres on answering questions that interest them. What is often less convincing is the common practice of presenting artificially real situations, which are remote from the lives and interests of children.

But do situations have to be *real* to be attractive? Fantasy or comedy situations can engage children's interest if presented imaginatively. The approach taken in Dutch schools, following the philosophy of Freudenthal, is translated as 'Realistic Mathematics Education' (RME). It typically begins a new topic by posing a problem in an interesting *realistic* context. This contrasts with the practice in English schools, where it is usual to use and apply the mathematical skill towards the *end* of a topic.

What is often not appreciated is that children's curiosity can be aroused enough to investigate patterns and relationships in mathematics itself. When this happens it is not the *relevance* as such that has raised the level of engagement, but rather the intriguing nature of the question that is posed.

References

Askew, M. (1999), *Issues in Teaching Numeracy in Primary Schools*. Buckingham: OUP.

Askew, M., Bibby, T., Brown, M. and Hodgen, J. (2004), *Examining Children's Opportunities To Learn Mental Calculation*. London: Beam Educational. www.beam.co.uk/pdfs/RES05.pdf (Accessed 1 October 2006.)

Croll, P. (1996), 'Teacher-Pupil interaction in the classroom' in P. Croll and N. Hastings (eds), *Effective Primary Teaching*. London: David Fulton.

Department for Education and Employment (1999a), *The National Curriculum: Handbook for Primary Teachers in England*. London: DfEE/QCA.

Department for Education and Employment (1999), *The National Numeracy Strategy: Framework for Teaching Mathematics from Reception to Year 6*. London: DfEE Publications.

Department for Education and Skills (2006), *Primary National Strategy: Primary Framework for Literacy and Mathematics*. London: DfES Publications.

Department for Education and Skills (DfES) 'Unit Plans.' www.standards.dfes.gov.uk/primary/mathematics (Accessed 1 October 2006.)

Department of Education and Science (1985), *Mathematics from 5 to 16*. London: HMSO.

Eddington, A. in Mackay, A.L. (1977), *The Harvest of a Quiet Eye*. Bristol: Institute of Physics.

Fosnot, C.T. and Dolk, M. (2001), *Young Mathematicians at Work: Constructing Number Sense, Addition and Subtraction*. Portsmouth, NH: Heinemann.

International Association for the Evaluation of Educational Achievement (2000), *TIMSS 1999 International Mathematics Report*. Boston, Mass: IEA.

Kyriacou, C. and Goulding, M. (2004), *A Systematic Review of the Impact of the Daily Mathematics Lesson in Enhancing Pupil Confidence*. Institute of Education, London: EPPI.

Piaget, J. (1970), *The Psychology of Intelligence*. London: Routledge and Kegan Paul.

Skemp, R. (1972), *The Psychology of Learning Mathematics*. London: Penguin.

Skemp, R. (1991), *Mathematics in the Primary School*. London: Routledge.

Straker, A. (1999), 'The National Numeracy Project: 1996-99' in I. Thompson (ed.), *Issues in Teaching Numeracy in Primary Schools*. Buckingham: OUP.

Teaching Mathematics: The Practice

5

Bob Davies

Although the teacher works within a variety of frameworks, s/he is the decision-maker every step of the way. Far from being strait-jackets, the frameworks within which s/he works provide the basis for the flexibility the teacher needs in order to tailor the learning experiences to the needs of her/his pupils.

(Jill Mansergh, Learning and Teaching Adviser, Mathematics)

Introduction: the debris from the strategies

The National Numeracy Strategy was a high pressure, high support curriculum development on a vast scale. In the initial stages considerable emphasis was placed on what could reasonably be a 'technology of teaching' – a system that reduced teaching to a small number of key elements, each with prescribed moves and devices. Although Strategy leaders were later keen to underline the flexibility that was available for teachers, many ideas emphasized by the Strategy may continue to be felt to be expectations upon teachers, even after their justification has been modified or replaced with different advice. Particular among these are:

- single learning objectives for a lesson
- three-part lesson structure, beginning with a mental/oral starter
- the use of fixed units of planning, with detailed scripts for each lesson prepared in advance, such as the Strategy unit plans.

The justification referred to was the 'informed prescription' to simplify and regularize the teaching of mathematics (as discussed in Chapter 4). It is the intention of this chapter to acknowledge the pervasiveness of such devices and suggest how the beginning teacher can both use such devices, and consider alternative organizational systems and thought structures. However, some limitations of the number of variables must take place when making decisions. Beginning teachers need models and structures to 'follow' and to work within – all teachers do. A significant impact of the Strategy was the increased confidence of primary teachers in teaching mathematics (Earl et al., 2003). Some of that increased confidence came from the security of following highly directive official advice, while some also came from the simplicity of the teaching model.

Earl et al (op cit.) warn that:

> ...some teachers may feel they have fully implemented the Strategies, but may lack awareness of the underlying principles (perhaps partly due to the early emphasis on the structure of lessons, e.g. the 'clock' in the literacy hour). Or some may lack subject knowledge that will limit their further improvements. Not knowing what they don't know, these teachers will have made the easier changes required by the Strategies and may not recognise that many changes and more knowledge are still required. (p. 94)

Nevertheless, with reflection upon their own experiences and further training in the specific pedagogy of mathematics, including the use of models, images and representations (see later in this chapter) and sources of mathematical misconceptions (DfES, 2005) – in short, many aspects of what Schulman (1987) called 'pedagogic content knowledge' – many schools are emerging as confident users of the support provided by the National Numeracy Strategy/Primary Framework for Mathematics in reaching their own decisions about teaching mathematics.

Planning

Preparing to teach mathematics

> You get to see the class in action; you see the teacher's planning; you see what happens in her lessons. There's only one lesson when you're really in the dark – the first time you teach yourself. You don't know what *you're* going to do. You know what the plan says, but you don't know the sorts of things you'll actually do.
>
> After the first time, you've got something to go on. You think, I could do that, or I could get one of the children to explain that.
>
> (Student reflecting on first teaching practice)

This comment clearly illustrates that, for all the wealth of support available for lesson planning, the individual teacher develops their own repertoire of possible 'moves' by which ideas are translated into action. Teaching is a dynamic interaction with a class of lively minds.

Planning formats and the elements needed in a lesson plan

Nearly all new teachers will easily adopt the lesson planning formats they are asked to use and make them work for themselves. Lesson plans are not, however, just for the teacher. Lesson planning formats can be considered part of a technology of monitoring and control of teaching, and it is appropriate to view these formats with a critical eye. The headings identified in a planning format preference some aspects of the preparation for a lesson over others. The pedagogic justification for each element of any such requirement should itself be explored.

Case study

A colleague recalls a pre-placement meeting with a student to look at the planning for the coming week (the first of the placement). On the front page, the date of the lesson was given, as was the learning objective: To explore number shapes. Other required detail was included briefly. In the format the university issued, the main body of the lesson plan is outlined on the other side. This part of the student's plan said: 'Why is 25 called a square number?'

This was followed by a large blank space, then: 'What other shapes could numbers have?'

There was nothing else.

Tutor: That's it?

Student: Yes.

Tutor: Hmm. Nice idea.

(Pause)

Tutor: Good questions. Is there anything else you might need to include?

Student: We could share and discuss outcomes in the plenary.

Tutor: Hmm. Why haven't you included any more detail about your role in the main part of the lesson?

Student: It depends what they say.

Tutor: Who?

Student: The pupils. It depends what they say.

Tutor: And are you ready for that – whatever they say?

Student: Well, I've done the maths.

Exploration of the aspect of mathematics to be taught and of the models and representations to be used in teaching must be one of the most valuable forms of preparation for teaching, and is what is referred to below as 'Do the Maths'.

Case study

Student teachers were asked to complete a preparation sheet, involving them in 'Doing the Maths' for a lesson to be carried out with 7- and 8-year-old children on investigating rectangular numbers. Afterwards they discussed the value of 'Doing the Maths'. One student suggested pooling their work.

At first, this was greeted with enthusiasm, and they began to devise systems for sharing their explorations. As they started to consider how they would then use the information made available, the doubts began to emerge: 'The whole point was doing it'; 'It doesn't take long, but you have to do it yourself.'

Within a few minutes of discussion, and without any input from the tutor present, the student who had made the suggestion summed up their deliberations: 'I didn't realize I made different connections from other people. It would be no good just looking at what other people have done, you need them there to talk through the way they see the maths.'

Something along the lines of the student's suggestion forms a part of the Japanese professional development approach called 'lesson study'. This involves the extended collaboration between teachers in the preparation of a lesson, which is then taught in the presence of other teachers and subsequently analysed in depth. The meticulousness of the lesson study process is explained in Fernandez and Yoshida (2004). The teacher in the lesson will seek to use interactive teaching in the sense advocated by Sugarman in the previous chapter, with 'searching, higher-order questions which seek to challenge and extend pupils' thinking and encourage a greater power to generalise' in a lesson about the calculation '12 – 7'. It follows a common format for Japanese lessons in which the students tackle a problem and then present and discuss their findings. Matsugaki (quoted in Fernandez and Yoshida, op cit: 228) illustrates how the interactive teaching engages all the learners:

> The intellectual confrontation that occurs during the student discussions fosters students' motivation to learn. In addition, the learning that occurs is deeper. In the student discussions, the students see the different ideas that were presented by others, they evaluate and rethink their own idea, and they think about strategies for convincing others of their ideas.

> In addition … as other students see the changes in that one student's thinking, they will,
> in turn, change how they see that student and will also start to change their own thinking.

The significance of the teacher's grasp of the subject knowledge now becomes clearer. In their 'Do the Maths' (author's term), the teachers anticipated the possible forms of the solution and, in preparation for their assessment for learning, even made a classroom layout plan to record which pupils used which forms of the solution.

Such detailed preparation for every lesson is unrealistic, but knowing the possible forms of the solution and understanding their mathematical structure will always be necessary if the teacher is to enable the pupils to go beyond saying what they did when they 'share outcomes'.

Strategies for teaching mathematics

Use of manipulatives ('resources'), models, images and analogies

The use of resources and models is explained thoroughly in Drews and Hansen (2007), and a useful selection of images is available on the DfES (2003) 'Models and Images in Years One to Three' CD-ROM.

Some representations, like number lines and hundred squares, are used frequently. Beginning teachers are advised to practise explaining using the empty number line, because its deceptive simplicity hides a vast range of small choices the teacher has to make. This is especially true when the teacher is seeking to represent faithfully a child's strategy. A very effective way of quickly developing this skill is to work with a colleague, sketching out each other's calculation strategies – one explaining, one drawing/writing – and then discussing the representation made.

Structured apparatus is equipment in which mathematical structure may be inherent in the design, such as base ten blocks made to represent the place value in our number system. Such apparatus may illustrate or reinforce concepts and relationships, but it does not teach them; and demonstrating the relationship between the apparatus and what it represents is not enough. The teacher needs to probe and challenge the pupils' understanding.

There is a danger with the use of structured apparatus that children learn to use the apparatus rather than the inherent mathematics. The apparatus may appear to the child as something to work with rather than as a source of insight. Everyday images have a greater immediacy and communicative potential – 'It's like the banister going down the stairs' (of a line graph) – that can be shared with others. The ability to see mathematics in things around us and to encourage children to do likewise is as important as familiarity with the available structured apparatus. There are mathematical representations everywhere, in arrangements of pieces of a bar of chocolate, the dates on a calendar and the angle formed when the door is open. Children can contribute these. Encouraging them to do so makes them more aware of the presence of mathematics around them and of their capacity to be mathematicians. Maths educators have identified the necessity of ensuring that learners experience a concept, such as that of 'rectangle', in a variety of ways in order to clarify the boundaries of the concept and avoid overly limited conception that arises from routinely experiencing the concept in a particular form. Again, however, this variety of experience is not enough on its own, as the following case study illustrates.

Case study

The teacher is beginning a lesson about rectangles with a Year 2 class (6- and 7- year-old children). She has given every child a small rectangle, and asks them to slide the rectangles around on their tables.

Every few seconds she says: 'Stop. What have you got on your table?'

They say: 'A rectangle.'

She draws then draws a rectangle on the whiteboard.

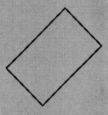

Teacher: 'What have I drawn?'

Child: 'A diamond.'

Several other children agreed.

The teacher could easily have forced through an acknowledgement that the shape was indeed a rectangle, but instead spent a considerable period of time encouraging the children to arrange the rectangles in different position on the table and to view the rectangles from different positions. What she did not do was to make the distinctive property of rectangles explicit. 'What can you see?' she asks. 'A rectangle' they all reply now, whatever the orientation of the rectangle. The teacher is satisfied that the children have had the corrective experience they needed. But she has not asked: 'How do you know it is a rectangle?'

Goswami (2001) warns that 'teachers need to present a series of examples of a particular concept within an explicit framework that emphasises relational similarity'. The teacher's own mathematical understanding is at a premium, however, so that the essential mathematical structure or relationship can be brought out clearly.

The teacher needs to know:

- that it is important for essential mathematical structures and relationships to be made explicit
- what the mathematical structures and relationships to be made explicit are in this case (Doing the Maths can be very helpful for this)
- how to make them explicit (asking the children what they know and how they know it to be correct will often be as good a strategy for this as any other).

Interactive teaching

The vital importance of high quality interaction between teacher and pupils when discussing mathematical ideas has been explored in Chapter 4. Interaction can be very effectively supported by use of electronic interactive teaching programs.

Using interactive whiteboards in teaching mathematics

Interactive teaching programs (ITP) give clarity and flexibility in the use of models and images, and support the use of ICT as a whole class teaching tool. When using this technology the emphasis is on effective whole class strategies, including teacher modelling, exposition and demonstration, prompting, probing and promoting questioning, class discussions managed by the teacher, and bringing the class together to reinforce key points emerging from individual and group work.

Some of the ITPs enable the teacher to make changes to the image displayed with greater clarity and speed than could be possible in any other way. The program 'Measuring Cylinder' is one such example. The program enables the container to be filled with different volumes and for different scales to be shown. The representation includes just the relevant detail. This is an example of a concrete representation that is showing only the essentials. Because of this, one may have reasonable expectation of transfer of understanding to the related idea of scale on the axes of graphs. In short, this program is a gem (www.standards. dfes.gov.uk/primary/teachingresources/mathematics/nns_itps/measuring_cylinder/).

However, many other ITPs, and much of the software prepared for teaching specific points, involve the use of representations that the teacher may be able to manipulate more effectively with pen and whiteboard or with the appropriate equipment.

What impact are interactive whiteboards having on the way teachers teach mathematics?

Using the interactive whiteboard or any projected material may tend to reinforce whole class teaching as a teaching approach (Higgins et al, 2005). This re-emphasizes the importance of the quality of the interactions. Interestingly, Higgins found that after a year of use, teachers using interactive whiteboards tended to focus their uptake or follow-up questions on the whole class rather than an individual child (p. 4). This suggests that pupils' responses were being used to involve other children in those lessons. Alexander (2000) noted the frequent failure of teachers in England to involve the whole class in the important teacher–pupil exchanges whereby key ideas were developed or clarified. It would seem that use of the interactive whiteboard militates against this weakness.

Assessing and monitoring progress in mathematics

Assessment for learning

Assessment for learning is the term given to 'the process of seeking and interpreting evidence for use by learners and their teachers to decide where the learners are in their learning, where they need to go and how best to get there' (Black and Williams, 1998).

It may sound self-evident, but the application of assessment for learning depends upon creating opportunities for assessment, i.e. creating the circumstances in which pupils may reveal their knowledge, skills and understanding. Additionally, several authoritative researchers have identified the importance of engaging the learners more specifically in the evaluation of their own performance, something that is only possible if the learners are encouraged to formulate or helped to share in the criteria by which their work may be assessed (see, for example, Wiliam, 2000).

Taken together with the processes of informal assessment, the term 'assessment for learning' has come to encapsulate nearly all aspects of sound teaching (DfES, 2004). Thus an aspect of the preparation for teaching, such as the clear specification of learning objectives, is considered to be part of assessment for learning because of the later assessment against these objectives. There is however a danger that when a term expands to refer to a whole set of interconnected ideas, it loses some of its explanatory power: and this may already have happened in the case of assessment for learning. This is simply an illustration of the complexity of teaching and how it is difficult (and not necessarily useful) to create simple categories of action.

Teacher trainers have always encouraged student teachers to modify their planning for later lessons in response to outcomes from earlier ones. The provision by the National Numeracy Strategy of 'sample' medium-term plans and, for most of Key Stage 2 at least, complete packages of weekly ('unit') plans for the whole year meant that students began to report that 'the planning has already been done'. More startling still has been the experience of some students who have been expected to teach Thursday's lesson plan regardless of what happened (i.e. of what the pupils learned) on Monday, Tuesday and Wednesday. This impression of inflexibility in planning was confirmed by Threlfall (2005), who found that teachers do not, on the whole, modify their planning between one lesson and another. Encouragement to retain and reuse planning from one year to another – validated as good practice under the workforce reform agenda – has reinforced this practice. This situation has been recognized by the DfES, whose guidance on using assessment formatively focuses instead on actions that the teacher can take in the course of the planned lesson (however the planning came about).

Particularly useful is the summary of ways of embedding day-to-day assessment strategies into learning and teaching (DfES, 2004: 44–5):

- questioning
- observing
- discussing
- analysing (with children)
- checking children's understanding
- engaging children in reviewing progress.

Case study: the assessment potential of different activities

Reflections on assessment for learning during a mental calculation unit of work:

an extract from an assignment submitted by Bryan Timms (Early Years part-time PGCE student), Bath Spa University, 2006.

One of the factors that had the biggest effect on the information I gained about the children's learning was the nature of the activity itself ... The activities varied in how much they allowed for the recording of the children's thinking. This was determined partly by how much freedom for exploration each activity offered. Below is a table summarising the main features and assessment issues of the delivered lessons.

Case study (continued)

	Organization	Equipment	Freedom to explore	Assessment potential
Lesson 1 **Dice game exploring + and – strategies**	Children played game in pairs on a 100 square.	100 squares Labelled dice (+9, +11, +19, –9, –11, –19)	No freedom to explore as children were asked to move their counters according to the dictates of the dice.	The activity did not produce written evidence. It had too many possible operations. It was modified and repeated for Lesson 4, based on the assessment that the task was both too complex and too restrictive.
Lesson 2 **Number stair investigation**	Children worked in small groups and individually. They were challenged to find and record as many number facts as they could.	Lego bricks arranged in steps to represent the numbers 1 to 10.	There were high levels of freedom to explore; the children could choose to work with facts such as 2 + 1 = 3 or with bigger numbers such as 7 + 3 = 10.	The activity produced a wealth of evidence, for example, some of the children had difficulty with placing numerals using the minus symbol (eg 3 – 7 = 4). Some surprising idiosyncratic and organized approaches were also demonstrated. **(Planned assessment)**
Lesson 3 **Bridging through ten**	Individual work. The children were asked to use a number line to practise partitioning strategies.	Number lines	There were some opportunities to explore, but these were limited by poor explanation of the activity.	Failed to produce substantial assessment information as children had to be guided too much in their completion of the task. Children's written work was not, therefore, a reflection of their understanding.

Case study (continued)

Lesson 4 **Adding tens and units**	As lesson 1, but children were asked to focus mainly on adding 11, and it was not presented as a game.	100 squares	Freedom for the children to explore. The children could work in any part of the 100 square that they chose. Many were fascinated by the operation of adding 11 to 89.	Activity provided useful written evidence. Most children attained the learning objective. A few exceeded the objective and extended the activity. One child was identified as needing particular support. **(Planned assessment)**

In later analysis, Bryan referred to 'the assessment potential' of different activities. This term has now passed into regular usage in preparation for school experience placements at the university.

Monitoring

Once pupil activities are successfully underway, the teacher must make a choice about how best to use this valuable opportunity. What should the teacher do – monitor the work of the class? Alexander (2000: 409) suggests that 'the word monitoring is more of a hindrance than a help, because its connotations of checking, policing and warning suggest activities a long way removed from teaching and learning'. Occasionally, particularly if the teacher has not explained some aspect of the task very well, it may be necessary to act as general class manager, policing and supporting as needs are identified, whatever the teacher had planned. However, it is often very valuable to work with a specific group for a sustained period.

Conscientious teachers may naturally feel that they should take every opportunity to intervene in children's learning and play a leading role when working with a group. Sometimes, however, it may be just as fruitful to observe and make only the occasional prompt. When the teacher decides that there is good potential for assessing a significant aspect of understanding, then he or she may move into active assessment mode. The teacher's understanding of the mathematics involved will influence the timing and quality of any such interventions, as in the following example.

Example: transcript of a classroom discussion

Jenny, Alex, Sam and Connor are explaining the ways they calculated 27 x 9.

Jenny: You draw a box to do it in *(points)*.

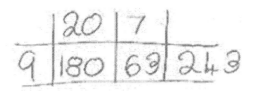

Jenny: I split the numbers up into tens and units. Nine is just units, so you only need one row.

(She explains each step of the calculation.)

Teacher: Now, can you tell me, what's 28 x 9?

(No response.)

Teacher: Is 28 x 9 more than 243 or less than 243?

(Sam clearly knows, so the teacher looks expectantly at him.)

Sam: More.

(The teacher glances at Sam's working. Sam has simply added 9 to his total, giving 252.)

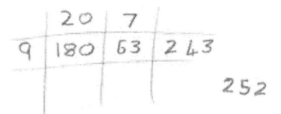

The teacher is in assessment mode at this point, so delays asking Sam to explain his strategy to the others. Instead, the teacher asks the others to complete the 28 x 9 calculation independently. Jenny, Alex and Connor all begin a new calculation.

Jenny's work is shown below. Her initial calculation is shown first.

Example (continued)

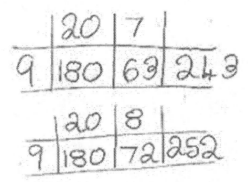

Alex and Connor work the calculation in the same way.

The teacher has (tentatively) identified the limitations of the pupils' knowledge of multiplication and switches into teaching mode for the remainder of the time with the group.

This assessment identified only one pupil who could use the information that 9 x 27 = 243 to find 9 x 28. Two important observations arise concerning the other two pupils in the group: they are getting their work right; and their limited understanding is only apparent when they are questioned in depth.

Before leading the pupils on to using even more sophisticated strategies and procedures for multiplying larger numbers, the teacher will need to help the pupils to appreciate the connections in what they know, and to use the knowledge they have more flexibly.

Taken from Davies (2005)

How children's learning in mathematics progresses and how to keep track of it

One attraction of objectives-based models of the curriculum lies in the ease with which the lists of objectives can form the basis of record-keeping systems. The assessment for learning model, linked with a mathematics framework's identification of sequential learning objectives, may suggest a fairly straightforward linear development, in which it is easy to identify next steps or targets. Again, the reality is more complex, and not just because you have to get the objectives 'right'. However, before going on to explore this complexity, a reality check is needed. It is not possible for teachers to assess all that they teach, or to respond to all the assessment information they might glean. Teachers and children have only so much time. Some things are more important than others

Teachers need to be able to:

- identify which objectives are the most important ones
- devise manageable and useful record-keeping systems.

These are likely to be judgements made by teams of teachers, drawing upon available guidance as well as upon their own experience and values.

A great practical strength of both the National Numeracy Strategy and the Performance Framework for Mathematics has been the identification of a small number of key objectives for each year. The value of key objectives is that these should be aspects of learning that are so significant that the teacher must strive to ensure that each child's progress in each key objective is monitored, and that action to enable the child to make as much progress as possible is prioritized.

By way of illustrating how frameworks are enabling for schools rather than restricting, let us consider Park Hall Primary's approach to the Primary Framework's strands (of learning objectives) for number and calculation. Park Hall (not its real name) has regrouped some of the objectives for calculating to align more closely with their perception of how calculation develops (and added one or two objectives of their own).

Primary Framework strands	School strands
Knowing and using number facts	Knowledge and recall of number facts and calculation procedures
Calculating	Confidence in transforming* numbers and calculations (* What the school means is perhaps best illustrated by the example of the 6-year-old who calculated 13 + 8 = 21 by counting 19, 20, 21. Think about it.)
Counting and understanding number	Counting in bigger chunks/understanding place value (x10, ÷10 etc.)

Figure 5.1 Park Hall's objectives for calculation

Having decided what they are looking for and how these elements contribute to the development of calculating ability, the teachers in the school are able to develop their own record-keeping system to give them the information they need. The teachers seek to identify how capable and confident children are in transforming calculations, because they believe this contributes greatly to mastery of effective calculation strategies. So this aspect of learning needs to be assessed (see below).

Demonstrated competence and what the child may know

We cannot confidently say what mathematics children understand, but we can observe what they do. For this reason there has been an increased emphasis on the demonstration of competence in assessment in recent years. Let us analyse through the eyes of the Park Hall teachers some assessment of the Primary Framework Year 4 'end-of-year' objective: 'Develop and use written methods to record, support and explain multiplication ... of two-digit numbers by a one-digit number.'

Case study

Consider three children who each successfully complete the calculation 35 x 8 = 280 independently, and can explain their methods to the teacher or teaching assistant. They have demonstrated their competence in this objective. But our teachers, trying however imperfectly to assess the children's knowledge and understanding, are not satisfied simply to record this as a demonstration of competence. The teachers briefly discuss the calculation methods used with each child *because they want the information that such explanations yield.*

- Child A uses the partitioning procedure by rote: 30 x 8 and 5 x 8. 30 x 8 is troublesome for her, but she knows it cannot be 24, so she opts for 240 and completes the calculation successfully.
- Child B doubles 35 to make 70, doubles it again to make 140, and again to make 280. None of these calculations required more than basic number knowledge.
- Child C calculates 35 x 10 = 350 as a guide, but cannot remember the procedure to use. She has a quick look back in her book and finds a similar calculation. Using this as a template, she uses the same procedure. The answer this yields, 280, matches her rough estimate so she is confident that she is correct.

Each child has different strengths and different needs that are not revealed by the correct answer of 280 in each case. Informal discussion and supportive questioning will reveal such strengths and weaknesses in minutes.

Differing paths of development of conceptual understanding and computational skills

In a recent study with many important outcomes, Gilmore and Bryant (2006) found that in some children the link between computational skill and the related conceptual understanding was much lower than one might expect. They found that 'a substantial subgroup of children exists, whose conceptual understanding far outstrips their arithmetical skill'(p. 328) (although they did not find a subgroup of children who show more advanced arithmetical skill than conceptual understanding). They conclude that teachers need to use a wide range of assessment strategies to uncover pupils' individual profiles of strengths and weaknesses, not just single measures of performance, in order to avoid the danger of some children being 'misclassified' on the basis of their low level of demonstrated competence in calculation, when in fact they had good understanding.

Non-linear progression in learning and using calculation strategies: Siegler's 'overlapping waves' model

Robert Siegler's many years of research into children's use of different calculation strategies revealed that children typically know and use multiple strategies for the same task, and that these strategies coexist as alternative possibilities for long periods, even if some strategies are much less powerful than others. Within a short time period (a few minutes), children may vary the strategies they use for identical kinds of calculation. As teachers often find to their dismay, a child may use a particular calculation strategy that the teacher wishes to share with other children, only for the child to offer a completely different explanation of the calculation they did.

Faced with this variability, Siegler (1996) suggested an overlapping waves model of progression in the use of strategies, with more powerful strategies eventually replacing less powerful ones, but only after long periods of coexistence and with some highly reliable strategies, like counting on one's fingers, being highly resistant to replacement. Siegler also identified three dimensions of progress that seem particularly important:

- learning and using increasingly powerful strategies
- becoming more proficient in the use of already known strategies
- becoming more proficient in the choice of appropriate strategies.

Following a detailed literature review, Siegler (reported in Siegler and Svetina, 2006) has concluded that the most significant influence on the rate of adoption of newly discovered strategies is the accuracy the learners gain from the use of a new strategy. Where increases in accuracy are large, new strategies are adopted rapidly.

Both Siegler's work and that of Gilmore and Bryant (op cit) suggest that models of learning and assessment that rely on checklists of sequential competences are naively over-simplifying learning in mathematics. Those models that seek to track and develop the learner's full range of knowledge, skills and understanding seem to be more faithful to what we know about children's learning: but the very complexity of that learning means that teachers will still have to simplify (though in different ways) in order to be able to act.

Conclusion

The relationships and structure within mathematics can make it a particularly pleasing area of knowledge to teach and to learn. At all times, children have relevant prior knowledge that can be used in new learning. Askew et al (1997) identified the following features of effective teachers' behaviour:

- valuing children's methods and outcomes
- sharing their own strategies for doing mathematics
- making connections between different aspects of mathematics explicit.

Whether in preparation for teaching, classroom interactions or in seeking to assess children's understanding, the keys to success in teaching primary mathematics seem to lie in the quality of the teacher's own understanding of elementary mathematics, and in his or her willingness to allow pupils to fully reveal their own.

References

Alexander, R. (2000), *Culture and Pedagogy: International Comparisons in Primary Education*. Oxford: Blackwell.

Askew, M., Brown, M., Rhodes, V., Johnson, D. and Wiliam, D. (1997), *Effective Teachers of Numeracy*. London: Kings College.

Black, R. and Williams, D. (1998), *Beyond the Black Box*. London: Kings College.

Davies, R. (2005), 'Group assessments in mathematics' in R. Davies (ed.), *Treasure Chest: Project Reports from the North West Shropshire Education Action Zone*. Shrewsbury: NWSEAZ.

DfES (2004), *Assessment for Learning*. London: DfES.

DfES (2005), *Wave 3 Mathematics: Supporting Children With Gaps in their Mathematical Understanding*. London: DfES.

Drews, D. and Hansen, A. (2007), *Using Resources to Support Mathematical Thinking*. Exeter: Learning Matters.

Earl, L., Fullan, M., Leithwood, K., Levin, B., Torrance, N. and Watson, N. (2003), *Watching and Learning 3: Final Report of the External Evaluation of England's National Literacy and Numeracy Strategies*. Toronto: Ontario Institute for Studies in Education, University of Toronto.

Fernandez, C. and Yoshida, M. (2004), *Lesson Study: A Japanese Approach to Improving Mathematics Teaching and Learning*. Mahwah, NJ: Lawrence Erlbaum.

Gilmore, C. and Bryant, P. (2006), 'Individual differences in children's understanding of inversion and arithmetical skill.' *British Journal of Educational Psychology* 76 (2),309–31.

Goswami, U. (2001), 'Analogical reasoning in children' in D. Gentner, K.J. Holyoak and B.N. Kokinov (eds), *The Analogical Mind: Perspectives from Cognitive Science*. Cambridge, MA: MIT Press.

Higgins, S., Falzon, C., Hall, I., Moseley, D., Smith, F., Smith, H. and Wall, K. (2005), *Embedding ICT in the Literacy and Numeracy Strategies: Final Report*. Newcastle: University of Newcastle upon Tyne.

Schulman, L.S. (1987), 'Knowledge and teaching: Foundations of the new reform.' *Harvard Educational Review* 7 (1),1–22.

Siegler, R. (1996), *Emerging Minds: The Process of Change in Children's Thinking*. New York: Oxford University Press.

Siegler, R. and Svetina, M. (2006), 'What leads children to adopt new strategies?' *Child Development*. 77 (4), 997–1015.

Threlfall, J. (2005), 'The formative use of assessment information in planning – the notion of contingent planning.' *British Journal of Education Studies*. 53 (1), 54–65.

Wiliam, D. (2000), 'Formative assessment in mathematics – the learner's role.' *Equals* 6 (1), 19–22.

Teaching Mathematics: Beyond the Curriculum

Bob Davies

Chapter Outline

Outstanding Schools

1.3. In these schools, children are engaged by learning that develops and stretches them and excites their imagination. They enjoy the richness of their learning – not just learning different things, but learning in many different ways: out-of-doors, through play, in small groups, through art, music and sport, from each other, from adults other than teachers, before school, after school, with their parents and grandparents, formally and informally, by listening, by watching, and by doing.

These outstanding schools make this possible because they offer rich, exciting programmes of learning.

(DfES, 2003: 9)

Introduction

Having discussed the principles underpinning the teaching of mathematics and examined the ways in which these principles may be translated into effective practice, this chapter will now explore wider opportunities for developing mathematical knowledge and understanding. We will consider cross-curricular links, and approaches to the teaching of mathematics beyond the constraints of the daily mathematics lesson.

Mathematics and cross-curricular learning and teaching

Mathematics has nearly always been taught as a distinct subject. Even at the height of popularity of cross-curricular planning in the 1970s and 1980s, most schools taught much of their mathematics separately. What is it that makes mathematics so distinct? Many educators have emphasized the coherent internal logic and structure of mathematics. And, a few obvious overlaps apart (see below), success in formal assessments does not require (or is even aided by) cross-curricular approaches to learning and teaching.

There are three *a priori* justifications for cross-curricular learning:

- Mathematics is an indispensable tool for other disciplines and human thought. Mathematics education should reflect the importance of mathematics, and what it can do.
- Application of mathematical knowledge and understanding is necessary if learners are to understand the connections and power of mathematics. To equip students with mathematical reasoning and better understanding of the subject, we must let them apply, relate and discover concepts.
- Knowledge of the world is interconnected. Subject divisions are arbitrary at best, and possibly unhelpful.

Mathematics as a tool, key skill or 'servant' subject

Some mathematics skills act as 'servants' of work in several curriculum areas, such as measurement (particularly in science), and data-handling in any aspect of the curriculum in which data is collected and/or analysed and interpreted. (For more about 'key skills', see www.dfes.gov.uk/keyskills.)

There are clearly advantages in identifying the inherent overlaps between mathematics and other subjects at the medium-term planning stage (see Figure 6.1).

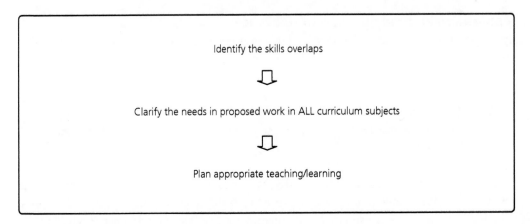

Identify the skills overlaps

Clarify the needs in proposed work in ALL curriculum subjects

Plan appropriate teaching/learning

Figure 6.1 The identify, clarify, plan model

However, just because a skill may be helpful in work in another aspect of the curriculum, it does not necessarily follow that the teacher should always plan to teach necessary skills in advance. In addition to the usual sequence of Learning Practice Application, there are other possible sequences, for example: Experiencing need Learning Application Further learning Practice.

Realizing the value of a skill may give an increased sense of purpose in learning. Learning to use a skill in context may challenge the learner to strive for mastery.

Case study

Some Year 3 and 4 children were learning about the properties of heat loss. The pupils tested the insulation properties of different materials in a way that will be familiar to most teachers. The teacher then helped the children to use data loggers to collect data for the temperature in each of the differently insulated cans over a period of time.

One pupil's equipment had not been connected correctly. Her graph was different from the others; it was straight. The horizontal graph raised many questions. It also helped the children to make comparisons.

These children gained experience of interpreting graphs of data they had collected and understood. They had not been taught about graphs in preparation. This experience would be valuable preparation for learning how to construct and use graphs later.

Application and the question of relevance

It is interesting to note that the only specific requirement for relevance to anything outside mathematics come in the sections of the National Curriculum Key Stage 2 Programme of Study for handling data (DfEE, 1999):

> *Problem solving*
>
> a) select and use handling data skills when solving problems in other areas of the curriculum, in particular science.

The importance of application of knowledge, skills and understanding, and in particular the significance of 'relevance' in learning mathematics, is discussed in some depth in Chapter 4. The issue is one that has exercised mathematics educators the world over. Reviewing the 'Math Wars' in the United States, Schoenfeld (2004: 11) writes:

> Research indicated that classroom instruction, which tended to focus almost exclusively on the knowledge base, deprived students of problem solving knowledge. It gave them little experience grappling with tough challenges, and fostered the development of numerous unproductive beliefs. (See de Corte, Verschaffel, & Greer (1996) and Schoenfeld (1992) for detailed summaries of the literature.) The research did not, in general, say how these problems should be fixed – but it did make it clear that such problems needed to be fixed. On the basis of what was known by the middle of the 1980s, it was clear that goals for mathematics instruction had to be much broader than mere content mastery. Students needed to learn to think mathematically as well as to master the relevant mathematical content.

What is increasingly clear is that in order to learn mathematics, learners have to think mathematically, and to behave like a mathematician. This, of course, prompts the more fundamental questions of 'What is mathematics?' and 'What is it that mathematicians do?': and Hersh's enigmatic definition that 'mathematics is what mathematicians do' (Hersh, 1998) may not be helpful enough. Stewart (2006) proposes instead: 'a mathematician is someone who sees opportunities for doing mathematics. I'm pretty sure that's it. It pins down an important distinction between mathematicians and everyone else' (p. 32).

This clearly implies the ability to recognize an aspect of mathematics in an unfamiliar context. But that unfamiliar context could be an unfamiliar context in the mathematics classroom, or in some aspect of mathematics. Relevance of an activity in mathematics may be achieved by activating interest in how one aspect of mathematics relates to another. (The need for interconnectedness of learning to be identified and developed *within* mathematics was a theme of Chapter 5.)

Returning to Schoenfeld's summary of the outcome of the Math Wars (above), we might conclude that there is no necessary reason why this behaving mathematically should be done better (or even as well) when mathematics is taught as part of a programme of cross-curricular learning. Some aspects of learning mathematics are probably better developed in discrete mathematics lessons.

In short, mathematical competence was shown to depend on a number of factors:

- having a strong knowledge base;
- having access to productive problem solving strategies;
- making effective use of the knowledge one has (this is known as 'metacognition'); and
- having a set of productive beliefs about oneself and the mathematical enterprise (which position the individual to act in mathematically appropriate ways).

There is also the third justification for cross-curricular mathematics.

Knowledge of the world is interconnected. Subject divisions are arbitrary at best, and possibly unhelpful

Distinct subject divisions are used in the specification of the National Curriculum, but *Excellence and Enjoyment* (DfES, 2003) makes clear that 'there is no requirement for subjects to be taught discretely – they can be grouped, or taught through projects – if strong enough links are created between subjects, pupils' knowledge and skills can be used across the whole curriculum' (p. 17).

However, in order to meet statutory requirements, any curriculum model will need to ensure progression in learning. And there is no let-up in the expectations for standards of performance in mathematics. From September 2006, primary schools have had revised frameworks for teaching literacy and maths. They are designed to support further increases in standards; and to reduce teacher workload and encourage more long-term planning (DfES, 2007).

When it comes to decision making, a school's interest in pursuing cross-curricular learning and teaching depends on what staff members consider to be the purposes of education. While there is no imperative for cross-curricularity from the drive to raise standards as measured by performance in national tests, there are other legitimate purposes for education, including critical inquiry into the world around us.

If children's capacity for critical inquiry is to be furthered, topics being studied must be located in a broader societal context, and this would be better supported by cross-curricular activities.

Does mathematics have any role to play in education for democratic equality and social justice and in preparation for citizenship?

The subject certainly can play such a role, but it comes about largely from using mathematics in the analysis of significant issues. Thus the teacher or children could conceivably use international data on political representation to create pie charts.

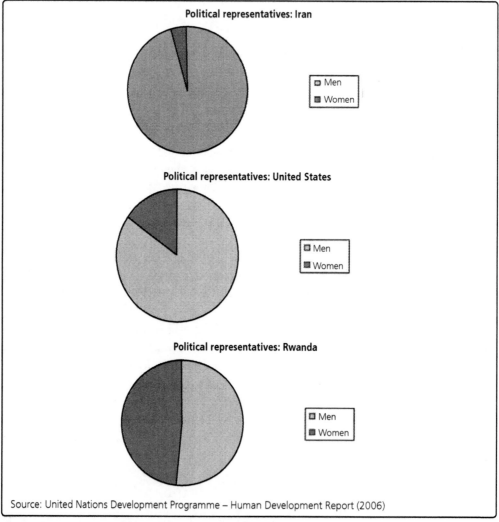

Source: United Nations Development Programme – Human Development Report (2006)

Figure 6.2 Using mathematics in preparation for citizenship

Whether teachers choose to make their curriculum relevant to the social issues of the wider world is still largely a matter of choice. In the absence of the security that official encouragement might give, a natural reservation from tackling anything too 'political' might be forgiven. However, this would still represent a deliberate choice to keep the wider world out of mathematics.

Relevance, real life and problem solving

There are many circumstances in which teachers or children might identify a possibility for acting mathematically. If these occur in the day-to-day activities of the school, the context or the purpose can provide both the shape of the problem and make it quite a challenge for the children to decide upon what mathematics to use. Consider these two examples, in which the problem-solver has to find all possible outcomes as part of the problem-solving process.

Example 1: from Key Stage 2 Tests Paper A (QCA, 2005)

Here are some digit cards.

| **2** | **4** | **6** | **6** |

Write **all** the **three-digit numbers greater than 500** that can be made using these cards.

One has been done for you: 626

The pupils will probably have encountered a 'problem' in a form very similar to this before. Through the use of the digit cards, the 'problem' is presented in its most abstract form, and the example 'done for you' ensures the pupils do not have to make sense of the task for themselves. They just have to remember to keep to the conditions clearly flagged up in bold text.

This reinforcement of behaviourist approaches epitomizes the impact of the national tests upon the primary mathematics curriculum. Contrast this with a problem situation that arose from preparation for a school Summer Fair.

Example 2: the Human Fruit Machine

The children plan to organize a Human Fruit Machine for the school Summer Fair. Three of the children will each have an orange, an apple and a lemon in a pouch tied round her or his waist. They can be accompanied by two other children: one who imitates the lever to operate the machine and provides the sound effects, and another who handles the money, including paying out for wins. To play, you pay your money and pull the lever. The 'machine' makes a lot of clanking and clunking noises, then each child pulls out a fruit (without prior consultation!). Three of a kind wins. The children have to decide how much to charge and how much they will pay out for three of a kind.

Observing how the children tackled this problem, the teacher learned a lot about the extent they could transfer their knowledge from one situation to another, as well about their skill in finding all possibilities and calculation probabilities. The problem required the children to investigate all possibilities and to calculate probabilities. The answers they reached informed their choices about cost and prizes.

Clearly, there is not a forthcoming Summer Fair every week. But some way has to be found of challenging children to select for themselves the mathematics needed. Some demand upon them to transfer learning can be achieved simply by breaking the closeness of the learn–practice–apply cycle. Askew and Wiliam (1995) noted that word problems (stories requiring translation into mathematical operations, also sometimes called 'standard problems') tend to be associated with situations in which children already know which operation to use – the children may have been practising precisely that type of calculation. They suggest that posing word problems without the prior signalling of what calculations may be involved can provide effective learning situations. There is a simple and powerful truth here.

So far as possible, such problems need be plausible and not contradict the common sense of the child with relevant knowledge (a question concerning tree heights and lengths of planks of wood that could be cut from them comes to mind). Indeed, setting the problems in a familiar context (for example, the exploits and daily habits of the teacher's cat), can be useful, particularly with younger children. It enables their prior knowledge to be activated. They can use their common sense. But it gives no clues about what mathematics they might need to do; they have to work that out for themselves.

This again links to the previous discussion of relevance. Teacher contrivance is no obstacle to the wholehearted engagement of children's interest. Once the teacher has engaged the children's interest, so that the problem has become a 'real concern' for them, it has all the merits that teachers seek to attach to 'real life' problems – whether the teacher (still) has a cat or not.

Note: If greater emphasis were to be given to teacher assessment in end of Key Stage assessments, as is the case in Wales, teachers would be able to arrange more sustained opportunities to assess children's abilities to transfer knowledge and to solve more significant problems.

Mathematics beyond the classroom

Links with the community – Extended schools
5.8. Extended schools support standards because they take a wider approach to supporting children's learning, with more opportunities for out-of-hours learning, and because they help build schools into the fabric of the local community. (DfES, 2003: 51)

There are many ways of providing additional out-of-hours opportunities for exploring mathematics:

- homework clubs – providing a space and time, with some adult supervision
- mathematics clubs – in which teachers and other interested adults encourage investigation
- support and booster sessions in mathematics for targeted children.

Although such forms of provision may be thought of as peripheral to the main business of primary education, they repay analysis not only for their own significance, but also for what such analysis may reveal about 'mainstream' teaching and learning.

Maths clubs

After school, lunchtime or holiday maths clubs provide an opportunity to offer different experiences of mathematics.

Opting in
Children attending mathematics clubs opt to attend them. They are likely to enjoy the activities not only because they have chosen them as something that interests them, but also because other children are also there because they want to be there.

Fun

An emphasis on enjoyment is a natural concern for those responsible for any voluntary additional activity. However, Askew (1998: 4) has wise advice on this topic (even though he is writing about in-school mathematics):

> Often people talk about the need to make mathematics 'fun'... Rather than mathematics being fun, it needs to be enjoyable and for most children being challenged is enjoyable ... and pleasure can arise out of meeting a challenge and reaching a satisfactory conclusion.

If a school recognizes children's lack of enjoyment of mathematics as a problem, then this needs to be addressed collectively, rather than by emphasizing the problem with a distinctively different approach in the maths club.

A different kind of mathematics?

Evans et al (2007: 4) suggest that it is because of the escape from 'the restrictions of a formal curriculum or defined teaching methods, and with no exam pressure on the participants' that maths clubs have their particular contribution to make. Are teachers really constrained and, if so, is some essential part of mathematics education being neglected?

Consider the DfES advice for ongoing activities to support mathematics in Year 6:

> The following is a useful checklist of key ongoing activities that can helpfully form part of your day-to-day mathematics/numeracy work with Year 6 children:
>
> - Use previous test questions as a teaching resource, linked to the curriculum focus for the week.
> - Model how to answer and annotate questions. Ensure children do this routinely when answering questions in class, not just for tests.
> - Use past Year 6 test questions in plenaries to highlight key learning points.
> - Use mark schemes to help children understand what and how much it is useful to record, e.g. to know when it is enough to write down just the calculation needed and when to show all the working out.
>
> (www.standards.dfes.gov.uk/primary/features/primary/supportforyear6/1107391, accessed July 2007)

This and similar guidance prioritizes for the teacher concern over how well the mathematics is being performed, over nurturing interest in mathematical dilemmas themselves:

> We would assert that one of the outcomes of the recent changes to the educational system in England is that schools focus so specifically on the act of learning mathematic that students often do not get a chance to experience what it is to do mathematics. (Pratt and Kelly, 2007: 34)

It may be that the significant contribution of maths clubs is that (with or without expert guidance) they can provide opportunities for children to use mathematics for their own purposes, whether this be in strategic thinking in a game, or in investigation or problem-solving. This is maybe a closer apprenticeship in becoming a mathematician than their habitual experience of school mathematics. This, of course, prompts the more fundamental questions of 'What is mathematics?' and 'What is it that mathematicians do?' that were discussed earlier in this chapter.

Young mathematicians will need support and guidance in whatever circumstances they do mathematics, but Stewart's definition that 'a mathematician is someone who sees opportunities for doing mathematics' (cited earlier) suggests the importance of the decision-making role of the young mathematician her- or himself in deciding what lines of inquiry or action to pursue. Such an approach is obviously problematic. Nevertheless, this digression, although prompted by discussion of the purpose of maths clubs, clearly raises further issues about the appropriate range of learning experiences for young learners of mathematics.

Working with parents

Harris and Goodall (2006), in a review of parental involvement research, conclude that there is a strong body of evidence to suggest that, whatever their own educational levels and abilities, parents have an important influence over children's achievement, through their impact on children's attitudes to learning and to school:

> There are many different forms of activity encompassed by the term 'parental involvement', but parental involvement in the form of 'at home' interest and support is a major influence upon educational outcomes.

There is a widespread negativity about mathematics among parents. The impact of such negativity is likely to be strongest upon lower achieving children, leading to a reinforcement of low expectations of achievement in mathematics. Parents do not want to encourage their children to be weak mathematicians, but if faced with negative messages about their child's performance their only supportive resource may be the commiserative, 'Well, I was no good at maths, either.'

The problem of calculation methods

Differences in calculation algorithms create tensions because, if parents' experience of learning maths was refining their use of specific algorithms, they are unlikely to be able to support children if they are using even slightly different forms of essentially the same method. However, because the number system is perfectly regular and because a little can be made to go a long way, children can be encouraged to use what they know. Encouraging the child to identify what they know and to try to use it to work out something else is the most useful thing one can do.

Conveying positive messages about mathematics and about children's achievements in mathematics

The review of learning at the end of a lesson can serve to locate that learning in a wider scheme of things. The teacher and/or the children can sum up the main learning that took place. While recognizing that knowledge is constructed anew in the mind of each learner should make us wary of assuming that the connections suggested by the teacher are those made by the child, it is surely helpful for the teacher to emphasize achievements and signpost links and applications. An additional benefit of the review/plenary may be that the pupil is able to make a more coherent answer to the question, 'What did you do today?' If the child is able to identify something positive about their mathematics learning, it enables the parent to make a positive comment in response. These things are cumulative. Positive attitudes develop slowly with much reinforcement needed.

Mathematics homework: issues in deciding what is suitable

Should practice exercises be set for homework?

'Consolidating skills and reinforcing understanding, particularly in literacy and numeracy' is one of the purposes for homework in the primary school identified in the DfES guidance (DfEE, 1998, still current). However, if such practice is to be challenging, then how will those needing help receive it? And if it is not challenging, then what is it for? An answer to this latter question may be that parents and carers will thereby find out about the calculation methods used in school, without the tensions that are likely to occur if they are unable to help children who ask for or need their help. If this is the intention, then it might be better to address this issue more directly through a Maths Evening and other contact and communication on the same topic.

Case study: not only the children learn from the homework that is set

One teacher, a bit shame-facedly, admitted two unexpected outcomes of their school's homework club:

- Improvements in the clarity of tasks and related information given to children for homework
- Discouraging teachers from setting calculation using a particular method as homework practice.

As in many other schools, their homework club is staffed on a rota system. At first, it was found that a major source of children's difficulties with their homework was not understanding what they were supposed to be doing. There are several reasons why this might occur, including the children not listening when they were being told. But supervising staff repeatedly found that they themselves could not work out what the children were supposed to be doing, and they began to mention this to the teachers concerned.

A telling problem arose with mathematics calculations, when pupils thought they had to calculate in a particular way. If they were no longer sure what this method was, it was now impossible for anyone to help them:

STUDENT A: I get it to 124. See, it's like this...
STUDENT B: Yes, but I'm not supposed to do it like that.

It was the *specification of the particular method* for the calculations that made the work so unsuitable as homework.

How might open-ended investigations be used as homework?

Open-ended investigations allow for participation at different levels, particularly if the early stages of the investigation are relatively straightforward (sometimes termed 'easy entry'), and hence are suitable for an occasional piece of extended homework, such as during a short school holiday. It is even better if the investigation generates plenty of attractive outcomes.

Starting the homework in the lesson can ensure that all children have a clear idea what to do. This is very valuable if the activity is something that may not be in a format familiar to parents: for example, an investigation into finding different triangles using a 3x3 dot matrix. The activity has easy entry, so all children will have outcomes to refer to at home.

Additionally, a prompt for how to extend the activity would give further support, as would an example. In this case the prompt might be: 'Children should try to identify triangles that are alike in some way, and, if possible, explain how they think the triangles are alike.'

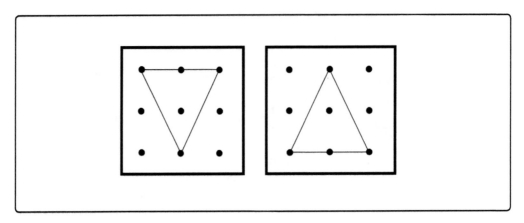

Figure 6.3 Identifying triangles on a 3x3 dot matrix

Pause to think

- How might the homework you set affect the attitudes of your children to mathematics?
- Are any of the children likely to struggle with the homework? If you know that when you set the homework, why are you setting it?
- Identify a particular child. Think about the homework you have set and the other communication you have had with the child's parent(s) or carer(s). What cumulative picture of your teaching and support for this child are you presenting?

Conclusion

In this chapter it has become evident that the teaching of mathematics, particularly open-ended investigations that build upon children's prior knowledge, can provide opportunities for worthwhile and meaningful learning of mathematics beyond the statutory curriculum. Liaison between teachers and those participating in such extended experiences will need to be effective and carefully planned. The outcomes, however, can be extremely positive, giving children and adults alike the opportunity to discuss and engage in mathematics in productive and non-threatening ways.

References

Askew, M. (1998), *Teaching Primary Mathematics*. London: Hodder and Stoughton.

Askew, M. and Wiliam, D. (1995), *Recent Research in Mathematics Education 5–16*. London: HMSO.

Becta (2003), *What the Research Says about Interactive Whiteboards*. www.becta.org/research (Accessed July 2007.)

Department for Education and Employment (1998), *Homework: Guidelines for Primary and Secondary Schools*. London: DfEE. www.dfes.gov.uk/homework (Accessed June 2007.)

Department for Education and Employment (1999), *The National Curriculum: Handbook for Primary Teachers in England*. London: DfEE.

Department for Education and Skills (2003), *Excellence and Enjoyment: A Strategy for Primary Schools*. London: DfES.

Department for Education and Skills (2007), findoutmore.dfes.gov.uk/2007/01/englands_nation.html

Evans, J., Nolan, K. and Hall, J. (2007), *Sum-it! How to set up your own maths club and keep it going*. www.continyou.org.uk/uploads/documents/doc_372.pdf (Accessed August 2007.)

Harris, A. and Goodall, J. (2006), *Parental Involvement in Education: An Overview of the Literature*. Coventry: University of Warwick. Available from www.schoolsnetwork.org.uk (Accessed July 2007.)

Hersh, R. (1998), *What is Mathematics, Really?* London, Vintage Books.

Pratt, N. and Kelly, P. (2007), 'Mapping mathematical communities: Classrooms, research communities and masterclass hybrids.' *For the Learning of Mathematics* 27 (2), 34–9.

Qualifications and Curriculum Authority (2005), *Key Stage Two Statutory Assessment Tests: Test Paper A Mathematics*. London: QCA Publications.

Schoenfeld, A.H. (2004), 'The Math Wars.' *Educational Policy* 18 (1), 253–86.

Stewart, I. (2006), *Letters to a Young Mathematician*. New York: Basic Books.

Teaching Science: The Principles

Susan Wright and Elaine Spink

Chapter Outline

Learning is for living, not merely for knowing.
(Hayes, 2006: 9)

Introduction

This chapter aims to inform you of the principles underpinning primary science education, to challenge you to consider your own practice in relation to these principles and to inspire you to translate the principles into effective practice (Chapter 8) and into broad, exciting and meaningful experiences of science that go beyond statutory curricula (Chapter 9).

The place of science in the primary curriculum

Let us begin by considering several definitions. Science is 'systematic knowledge of the physical or material world gained through observation and experimentation'; 'knowledge gained by systematic study' (Random House, 2006). Or perhaps it is 'Nothing more than trained common sense' (Thomas Henry Huxley, 1870, in Wolpert, 1992) – although this is a view vehemently refuted by many scientists and philosophers. Possibly nearer to reality is:

> ...an interrelated network of ideas, perceptions and processes in which there is an underlying requirement of consistency and that the whole enterprise makes sense (although not 'common sense'). (Goodwin, 1994: 8)

With so many different definitions comes the inescapable message that 'science' means different things to different people. Finding a precise definition which is satisfactory to all is not the issue (and is not likely to be possible). What we must recognize is that we all hold views about science derived from our experiences, and that these views are not based on formulating definitions of the word *per se* but on our conceptions of its nature. As teachers – and indeed as science educators – it is particularly important that we explore our views:

> ... the widely held, often unstated and to some extent unconscious assumptions about science and science education, whatever these assumptions may be, exert a strong influence upon the way we educate, the way we do science and the way we research into science education. (Stenhouse, 1985)

Read the following two conceptions of science, presented very eloquently and succinctly by Peter Medawar, and consider which accords best with your experiences. (It is interesting to note in this piece of writing that the use of 'man' to indicate a scientist reflects its time, 1967: but the content defies dating.)

Two conceptions of science

1. Science is above all else an imaginative and exploratory activity and the scientist is a man taking part in a great intellectual adventure. Intuition is the mainspring of every advancement of learning and 'having ideas' is the scientist's highest accomplishment.

2. Science is above all else a critical and analytical activity; the scientist is pre-eminently a man who requires evidence before he delivers an opinion and when it comes to evidence he is hard to please: it can speed thought but cannot start it or give it direction. (Medawar, 1967)

The conception which you prefer may well reveal the period during which your education in science took place. However, what is also fascinating is that our stated views about the nature of science and science education may not be displayed in our teaching of science. How many teachers espouse science as an imaginative and exploratory adventure and then deliver a critical, analytical and procedurally rigid experience of it to pupils?

As is so often the case, it may be that taking up a position 'on the fence', drawing on what is effective from both sides, is actually the most professionally useful place to be. Medawar also acknowledged that both conceptions accorded with experience:

'…anyone who has actually done or reflected deeply upon scientific research knows that there is in fact a great deal of truth in both of them. There is poetry in science but also a lot of book-keeping' (op cit).

Given then that 'science' is an intellectually – and frequently emotionally – loaded word, there have been attempts to better encapsulate what we try to provide for pupils. 'Knowledge & Understanding of the World' was coined by England's Department for Education and Skills/Qualifications and Curriculum Authority (DfES/QCA) to describe Early Learning Goals for children aged 3 to 5 (2000). This area of learning encompassed a broader range of what we would recognize as 'subjects' than only science (design technology, history, geography), but far better describes educators' attempts to do more than pass on a set of facts (knowledge). In Northern Ireland, the revised curriculum seeks to link subjects by themes, such as 'The World Around Us' (Department of Education Northern Ireland, 2007). In Scotland, a major review of the curriculum is underway and will create for the first time 'a seamless curriculum from age three to age eighteen, offer pupils greater choice and opportunity and give teachers more professional freedom' (Scottish Government, 2006). Again, the curriculum will be defined by broader themes, such as sustainability and topical science.

These areas of learning convey so much more than biology, chemistry and physics – far better to view science as 'life, the universe and everything' (Adams, 1979). However, as we move further into the twenty-first century it is even more important to recall Alan Goodwin's definition: 'an interrelated network of *ideas, perceptions* and *processes.*' The pace of change is such that it is not appropriate (was it ever appropriate?) to teach science as a collection of facts or a body of knowledge. The knowledge develops rapidly, it is never static and no sooner have we learned something than our learning could be obsolete. Knowledge is more 'available' than it has ever been before. The internet has ensured that for many, the answers to our questions are only clicks away. What then should we be 'teaching' our children, in science or indeed in any curriculum subject?

For children who reached the age of 5 in 2008, it is estimated that over 60 per cent of the jobs they will do as adults have yet to be invented (Barrett, 2006). The implication is clear: we must educate for change and equip children with the skills and attitudes not only to cope with change but to lead it. In science, this involves taking a closer look at the notion of scientific literacy.

Science education has to fulfil two purposes: one, preparing future scientists and technologists; and two, providing all young people with sufficient knowledge and understanding to become informed citizens (Harlen, 2006b: 6):

> If for every student who learns that they can 'do science' there have to be three or four who learn that they cannot, then that form of education is indefensible. (Claxton, 1991)

Many writers and science educators (Harlen and Qualter, 2004; Ratcliffe and Grace, 2003; Millar and Osborne, 1998) have put forward convincing arguments for the goal of science education to be scientific literacy, i.e. for all citizens to be able to *interact* with the science around them, questioning, considering evidence, applying knowledge and skills, and making informed decisions. They will learn that they *can* 'do science' and will be empowered to contribute; to hold and express opinions on issues; to critically respond to media claims; to seek and also understand the rationale underpinning advice given to them. For these reasons, it should be an entitlement for all learners. Scientific literacy develops as much from *how* you teach as *what* you teach, being notoriously difficult to proscribe in a curriculum. Its development will be enhanced by your acceptance of the tentative nature of scientific knowledge, and by your acknowledgement of its breadth of influence in every aspect of our lives.

The historical development of science in the primary curriculum

If we were to attempt to describe one 'typical' primary science lesson in 1970 and one from 2007, what similarities and differences would we see? It would be tempting to emphasize the differences and envisage a 1970 lesson in which the teacher directed and instructed the whole class, probably on an aspect of biological science and one that could have been linked to a 'nature walk' undertaken by the class previously. The teacher would draw the featured items and write the accompanying paragraph of description/explanation for the pupils to copy. In 2007, our imaginary teacher would be facilitating the purposeful activity of small groups of children. The children would be investigating a question they have raised themselves, using resources selected by them and recording as they saw fit. Learning would be constructed through communication and interaction.

Such images would be a gross simplification. At all times, there have been teachers who enabled their pupils to learn through meaningful activity and who exemplified science as the 'adventure' described by Medawar, comprising imaginative and exploratory activity. However, there have been recognizable trends in science education, and these have shaped the pathways we now follow.

UK curriculum projects in the 1960s and 1970s (such as Nuffield Junior Science and Science 5–13) encapsulated thinking about the value of involving children practically in enquiry, being creative in teaching approaches and drawing science from relevant contexts. Similar projects espoused similar aims in the USA and Australia. However, there was limited implementation, and this again was mirrored across continents. For example, a study in the USA reported that 70 per cent of school districts were not using any of the materials of the major curriculum projects (Weiss, 1978, in Harlen, 2006b: 5).

During the 1980s research gathered pace into the importance of children's ideas and the links between constructivism (see next section) and science education. Osborne and Freyberg, working in New Zealand, presented a framework in the Learning in Science Project (1985), which accorded with the findings and recommendations of the highly influential Children's Learning in Science project (CLIS) led by Rosalind Driver in the UK. The CLIS project (1982–9) identified preconceived ideas expressed by children from all parts of the world. The findings were incorporated into an approach to teaching that begins with the premise that teaching must start from the current ideas of the pupils. This project overlapped with the passing of the Education Reform Act in 1988. For the first time, the teaching of science was required (by consent in Scotland and by statute in the rest of the UK), and the content was prescribed. The resulting National Curriculum for Science in England has determined the content of science teaching since then (DfEE/QCA, 1999).

The SPACE Project (Science Processes and Concept Exploration, 1990–8) was among the first large-scale *primary* science-focused research projects. It highlighted the importance of working with children's ideas, emphasized the significance for learning of investigation, and showed how constructivist principles could be applied in primary science learning and teaching. It undoubtedly influenced proceeding curricular reviews in the UK.

A National Curriculum for science did not, of course, transform science teaching overnight; but much has been achieved in the intervening years. Primary science teaching and pupils' performance have improved significantly since the introduction of the National Curriculum in England and Wales, and children tend to be enthusiastic towards science at a young age (Parliamentary Office of Science and Technology, 2003). However, the concerns raised in this same report – that advances made in the early years of the National Curriculum for science were in danger of being lost – appear to have gained credence. In 2006, the annual report of Her Majesty's Chief Inspector of Schools (in England) reported that overall achievement in science was falling, with pupils lacking the knowledge and skills necessary to undertake investigations and make links between different areas of science (Ofsted/HMI, 2006).

Interestingly, as the National Curriculum tests for science in England (widely known as the SATs) have placed increasing emphasis on scientific enquiry-based questions, rather than the recall of science knowledge, so has attainment in these tests declined. Ofsted acknowledge that:

> At the heart of good achievement in science [is] active engagement of pupils in scientific enquiry. Some of the best achievement was found where pupils were taught well and were given opportunities to research topics, come up with their own ideas, exchange views, plan and carry out investigations and evaluate their work and that of others. (op cit)

So a National Curriculum and a nationally imposed system of assessment, testing and inspection can be a force for good, by ensuring those essential principles (discussed later in this chapter and in Chapter 8), many of which were highlighted by the science curriculum projects of the 1960s to 1990s, *have* to be implemented. That suggests a somewhat cynical stance – that pedagogy will be most influenced by an external imperative: when what really lies at the heart of curriculum development and pedagogical change is the welfare and well-being of the child. This has been enshrined (in England) in the five principles of *Every Child Matters* (DfES, 2004) to which every aspect of teaching and learning, in every subject and in every school, will contribute. The boundaries are blurring: between subjects, between facilitators of learning, between institutions and between professionals working with children. This can only serve to increase the potential for science to feature more broadly in the education of the individual and society.

More specifically, what is next for primary science education? The emphasis on first-hand experience, enquiry and investigation is set to continue. Added to this will be an increasing focus on personalized learning:'maintaining a focus on individual progress, in order to maximise all learners' capacity to learn, achieve and participate' (Training and Development Agency, 2007: 5). The trends will bring together what we have learned over the last 30 years about the importance of involving children in self-assessment, encouraging and enabling reflection on learning and promoting talk between learners (Harlen, 2006b: 8). Supporting primary teachers in making this shift will be a theoretical framework developed over many decades.

A theoretical framework for the teaching of science

We cannot identify or discuss all the theoretical views or frameworks that have influenced science teaching over the last 30 years. They are numerous, overlapping, and some have not stood the test of time. However, it is important that we consider the views that have had the most influence, or are likely to have the most influence in the future.

Arguably, the only way to move on with our teaching is to be open-minded and consider alternative viewpoints. Existing theories are being revisited, adapted, applied and re-applied to new contexts and new configurations of education.

Personal philosophy plays an important role as, either consciously or subconsciously, it will shape or determine the effectiveness of our teaching. Knowledge of how approaches to science teaching and learning developed, together with reflection on our own experiences and practices, encourage the creative thinking that enables us to move beyond received wisdom.

It would be simplistic to regard the history of educational philosophy as a menu from which to select our preferred 'dishes'. However, experience has shown that the most effective science teachers appear to be those most skilled in making that selection of dishes or elements from the range of models and theoretical frameworks available to them, and applying those elements in a flexible way.

Key themes that emerge in the research are constructivism (including social constructivism), and the significance of children's ideas. Equally significant, and with particular resonance to current thinking, are the themes of scientific enquiry (see Chapter 8), creativity, and moves towards personalized learning.

Constructivist approaches

Constructivism portrays learning as an active process in which learners construct new ideas or concepts based upon their current knowledge or prior experiences.

We are almost too familiar with Piaget, Bruner, Vygotsky – or are we? What relevance do they hold for understanding learning in science? They were all, broadly speaking, constructivists; but they represent at least three constructivist traditions: educational constructivism, (Piaget), personal constructivism (Bruner) and sociological constructivism (Vygotsky) (Matthews, 2000). This breadth undoubtedly poses problems in attempting to understand its complexities and to extrapolate implications for the teaching of science. But few would argue that 'The most conspicuous psychological influence on curriculum thinking in science since 1980 has been the constructivist view of learning' (Fensham, 1992: 801), reason enough for familiarizing ourselves with the key players and key messages.

Piaget acknowledged the sequential nature of learning based on the careful observation of children's conceptual development. He was, perhaps, bringing the child to the forefront of the learning process, where previously education had been largely based on assumptions and transmission. His views also turned the focus onto the individual. Conceptual development for each individual was viewed by Piaget as a series of stages, from pre-operational to formal thinking. It is this step progression that has been most influential, feeding forward into the constructivist and social constructivist views that followed.

Piaget's views have been subject to strong and well-publicized criticism (Donaldson, 1978), and there have been questions raised about the usefulness of a staged approach. For example, Roden (2005) suggests that the Piagetian influence on ages and stages significantly hindered the development of science through the 1970s and 1980s. However, it is remarkable that a model of learning that is almost 100 years old is still evident in today's schools.

Lev Vygotsky, a contemporary of Piaget's, viewed learning as a social process, and education as a vehicle for social transformation:

> Every function in the child's cultural development appears twice: first, on the social level, and later, on the individual level; first, between people and then inside the child…All the higher functions originate as actual relationships between individuals. (1978: 57)

His socio-cultural view gave rise to the notion of scaffolding, further developed by Bruner. When as teachers we decide upon what the next step should be for a particular child and enable them to take that step, Vygotsky would say we have identified the 'zone of proximal development', which is the area just beyond current ability or understanding. By 'scaffolding' the child's learning – through our questions, input and provision of experiences – we enable the child to take that next step towards more advanced ideas and skills.

For example, a 7-year-old child, on having his or her attention drawn to a puddle of water that has evaporated, may state that the water has simply 'gone' (SPACE, 1991). This notion seems to fit comfortably with what many teachers feel science education is about in these early stages of the twenty-first century: supporting children in developing their ideas and skills. However, as Harlen (2006a: 158) points out, a warning has to be given: 'Research…found that teachers could "talk scaffolding", but appeared to implement it only marginally…Scaffolding is not an excuse for telling children the "right answer".'

A third lasting legacy of Vygotsky's work was his views on the importance of language in learning and the links between language and thought. These were discussed in Chapter 1.

Bruner was influential: by seeking to build on child development research (particularly Piaget's) and on knowledge construction as an *active* process frequently involving others through dialogue (echoing social-constructivist views), he attempted to bridge domains within constructivism. He is most frequently associated by teachers with his model of a spiral curriculum, which is organized in such a way that the learner can continually build on what has gone before.

Children's ideas

Each facet of constructivist approaches views the learner as bringing existing ideas to bear on new situations; as extending and developing ideas and knowledge in the light of new experiences; and as actively constructing a view of the world (Peacock, 2000: 8) At the heart of this process are learners' ideas.

Fortunately, the 'jugs and mugs' approach to science teaching is coming to be seen as just as inappropriate as the *tabula rasa* view of children in education more generally (less common, but it still occurs). 'I, your teacher, am brimming over with expert knowledge' – the jug – 'and will endeavour to fill you, my pupils, who know very little if anything about this subject, with my knowledge by pouring it in'! All learners bring to all learning situations their own ideas, based on their previous experiences of the world and its phenomena. Even a newborn baby is rich in experience of the world inside the uterus, its sights, sounds, tastes and sensations. Who can say what ideas these experiences translate into for a newborn: but innate ideas can be seen to be applied within minutes of a baby beginning its independent life. From the moment of birth, a baby has the ability to follow an idea, probably a smell-based idea, unaided by adults, by wriggling to the mother's nipple and achieving her or his first fast-food takeaway. However, it is also true to say that as a result of a baby's or a child's more limited experience of the world, many of the ideas or conceptions they form will not accord with the accepted scientific view. It will be an 'alternative construct', or what is more commonly referred to as a misconception.

Pause to think

Discuss the following statements with a colleague and explain why they are misconceptions. What kinds of discussions and/or activities could you include in your teaching to address these misconceptions?

- we see things because light comes from our eyes and lights them up
- sugar melts in water
- people are not animals
- heavy things sink
- trees and bushes are not plants
- a light bulb uses up electricity.

(Adapted from Teachernet, 2007)

These ideas/misconceptions can be very strongly held and resistant to change. So if, as writers such as Sharp (2004), Harlen and many others would have us believe, developing *understanding* of concepts in science (rather than only acquiring knowledge of those concepts) depends on replacing these misconceptions with scientifically accepted alternatives, the teacher has a difficult task on her or his hands.

You, the children's teacher, must enable ideas to be expressed, discussed, tested and evaluated as appropriate. There are many resources and publications to support you in this (see for example Keogh and Naylor's 'Concept Cartoons', 1999) But to return to the proviso 'as appropriate': Why the qualification? Rigorous application of constructivist principles to primary science teaching, such as those advocated by the SPACE Project research, has proved very difficult to achieve. Teachers point to the plethora of ideas emanating from their pupils or, conversely, the seeming lack of ideas about a particular event or object. Asoko (2002) offers an alternative position, which appeals to teachers because it appears to fit more comfortably with what they know to be effective. She suggests that rather than work *from* children's ideas, we work *with* them, with our teaching informed by knowledge of the misconceptions likely to be present.

We have been talking here about 'learning' when what we set out to do was to explore effective *teaching* of science. What might these frameworks, theories and models look like in practice – in *effective* practice?

Principles of good practice

The quotation that started this chapter, 'Learning is for living, not merely for knowing' (Hayes, 2006: 9), is at the forefront of many recent changes in education, implicitly if not explicitly. This is reflected in current government policies and developments, and these in turn have been influenced by existing theoretical views.

The question of how these views are turned into practice has long been considered, and the following elements emerge time and again as features of effective practice:

- creating an inclusive environment
- valuing children's ideas
- the 'hands on', active involvement of learners
- creativity (both teaching creatively and teaching for creativity)
- developing communication skills: specifically, enabling 'talk' to happen
- variety in teaching and learning approaches
- an emphasis on the development of skills and attitudes.

These elements are identified not only by researchers and teachers, but by children.

Example

What do children say in response to questions about what makes a 'good science lesson' and a 'good science teacher'?

- 'When there are loads of experiments and we do them.'
- 'She uses the Smartboard.'
- 'When we do science about things we like – cheese, chocolate and crisps.'
- 'He listens to me.'
- 'I feel I can talk.'
- 'I love it when I can discover things with my group and we get to tell the rest of the class but not write it down though.'

The enthusiasm generally professed for science among children aged 4 to 12 seems to suggest that we are 'on the right track' as far as children are concerned.

So, what will the effective teacher of science actually be *doing*?

Contextualizing

This means acknowledging that a meaningful context is very important to learning. The teacher will provide learning experiences or resources or activities that are meaningful and relevant to the children because, for example, they are recognizable, they are a part of daily life, they are based on a shared experience.

Generally, the younger the child, the 'closer' to them we need to locate the experiences offered. As children get older, then their world and experiences can expand. It can be useful to envisage this as a series of concentric circles, with the youngest children being provided with experiences within a familiar and recognizable context, and the range of contexts and experiences gradually expanding and increasing in complexity as they grow older. For example, the environment of concern and interest to me as a 3 year old is the room I am in. Later, the environment encompasses my home, my street, my village, my country and so on, perhaps to the ends of the universe. This is not to say that young children should not be exposed to activities that are outside of their experience: variety is the spice of life, and also of science teaching and learning!

Signposting

It is necessary to know where you have been in order to know where you are going. To this end 'signposting' is considered good practice, and many teachers recap with their class upon previous learning and experiences and explicitly share learning intentions and objectives. This makes the 'bigger picture' more accessible, and knowledge acquisition less fragmented.

A National Curriculum imposes judgements about what is and is not suitable subject content for learners of particular ages. Schemes of work based on this (such as England's Scheme of Work for Science: QCA/DfEE, 1998) may contribute to the fragmentation of knowledge. Units may be used in isolation and considered to 'stand alone':

> The school science curriculum is failing to construct a coherent picture of the subject, its methods and its practices, leaving pupils with fragmented pieces of knowledge. (Osborne and Collins, 2002 in Duggan and Gott, 2002: 30)

Consider a teacher who takes the class outside to look at a puddle disappearing, or ice melting. What is actually happening? The specified intention might be to introduce or consolidate scientific vocabulary such as evaporation, condensation or melting – the curriculum requires that children know these terms. But the 'big idea' is overlooked. This 'big idea' or over-arching principle is particle theory, a powerful explanatory notion of great importance in the scientific world: yet it is not explicitly expressed because it does not feature in the statutory curriculum. Primary-aged children are certainly capable of role-playing particles in an ice cube, undergoing changes of state, modelling movements and bonding, and so envisaging what happens when water evaporates, condenses or freezes. Why not help the children to make those links, regardless of statutory obligations?

Signposting will prepare children for the next steps in their learning and will lay the foundations for what is to come.

Promoting scientific enquiry

Where does scientific understanding come from?

> [It] proceeds, develops and changes by questioning the validity and reliability of scientific 'truths' often accepted as scientific 'facts'. (Roden, 2005: 46)

That is, understanding emerges from the science process. As Roden goes on to say, echoing the views of science education researchers across the world, it is therefore appropriate – and necessary – for children to engage with science in this way, posing questions, testing hypotheses, forming explanations and questioning judgements. They must *enquire scientifically.*

A distinction needs to be made between scientific enquiry and 'practical work'. An investigation requires more than the use of equipment and the carrying out of practical tasks. Both teachers and children need to have an explicit focus and know what they are hoping to achieve. The learning outcomes of a science activity should be more frequently related to the skills and attitudes of scientific enquiry than to subject knowledge. There is strong evidence that the highest standards are seen in schools where schemes of work are well integrated with scientific enquiry (Richardson in Harlen, 2006b: 142).

Encouraging and planning for child-centred discussion

This is at the heart of good practice and, arguably, of the dominant theories already discussed. The potential is enormous: to create a climate of enquiry, where ideas, questions and discussions are welcomed and all ideas are valued can lead to great things. This was the culture in the laboratories of Watson and Crick of DNA fame, where a member of the team said: 'There was no shame in floating stupid ideas' (Ridley, 2006). By encouraging discussion the teacher can enable children to be involved in their learning, giving them some control and developing their thinking skills. What we know of children's learning in science emphasizes the need for choice – for children's choices. This increase in learner autonomy can be viewed as threatening by some teachers. Initial teacher trainees we have worked with, who were science specialists in the third year of their degree studies, found this notion 'very scary' and were initially hostile to the idea of 'letting the children take the reins'. However, after they had experience of teaching in this way, applying the TASC approach (Thinking

Actively in a Social Context – for more information see Belle Wallace, 2002), many found it difficult to imagine teaching in any other way.

There is also an opportunity, via discussion, to actively involve children in assessing their work. They can self-assess, peer assess, discuss success criteria... the list is almost endless. Child-centred discussion, particularly that focused on assessment, strengthens personalized learning.

Modelling

This is an important way to achieve what you want – that is, excellence in teaching and learning. It involves acting in ways that children will aspire to, both explicitly and implicitly, or showing them skills that need to be developed, 'serving as an example to be imitated or compared' (Oxford English Dictionary). So, it can be applied on two levels: modelling skills and modelling attitudes. Both are important and can impact positively upon learning. As Harlen (2006a: 96) points out, 'skills' and 'attitudes' are essential components of the complex activity of enquiry or investigation. An enthusiastic teacher who wonders about the world and its phenomena, who is open to ideas, who values questions and models what we can do with our questions, will inspire confident, independent learners with positive attitudes towards science – a legacy worth striving for.

We have examined several of the components of effective teaching in science. We also know some of the elements of less effective practice: a reliance on worksheets; copying from the teacher's writing; overemphasis on recording and writing; imparting of 'facts' by emphasizing the knowledge component of science; teacher-dominated talk and decision making; and lack of learners' choice. There are certainly others – you will be able to add to this list from your own experiences.

What the teacher needs to know

All will agree that the teacher needs to be knowledgeable: but knowledgeable about what exactly?

As we have previously discussed, because the bounds of knowledge are constantly expanding and national curricula are constantly changing, effective science teaching today requires the teacher to be knowledgeable *not* about the content of the subject. Rather, it requires knowledge of:

- how to find out (personal research skills)
- how to teach (pedagogy and the principles of good practice)
- how to intervene effectively, in order to 'scaffold' children's understanding

- how to differentiate effectively, to meet the learning needs of all children (this links directly with the personalization of learning).

Science education is best regarded as a conceptual journey, undertaken by learners and their teachers. The right answers are less important than the journey itself; and the right answers that we have today could change tomorrow.

However, there is a very real tension or mismatch here. This is because many people, including the teaching community, regard science as being largely concerned with 'right answers'. When teachers perceive that they do not know the 'right answers' they may lack confidence in their ability to teach the subject effectively. Accepting that the notion that 'science and scientists can explain everything' is a misconception is vital for progressing confidently in science education.

With regard to the subject knowledge that teachers of science need to have, there have been many attempts to define this and to distil science knowledge into a set of key ideas. It is true that 'big ideas' exist – they are ideas that are widely applicable and that make links between explanations and occurrences, forming broad theories or accepted principles. There is, however, less agreement about what and how many ideas qualify as those fundamental to understanding. One attempt is represented by the Key Stage 3 National Strategy for Science in England (DfES, 2002): and the ideas this identified have underpinned curriculum reviews since. According to the strategy, the five key scientific ideas are: cells; interdependence; particles; forces; and energy. We could extrapolate from this that if these ideas are crucial for an effective education in science, then teachers need to be familiar with the concepts associated with those five areas. The Professional Standards for Teachers in England (TDA, 2007) do not prescribe the content of teacher subject knowledge, the lessons having been learned from previous attempts to do so! Rather, professional judgement and expertise is brought to bear. The standards require that teachers:

> Have a secure knowledge and understanding of their subjects/curriculum areas and related pedagogy to enable them to teach effectively across the age and ability range for which they are trained. (Q14)

Science subject ideas that are appropriate for the primary (5 to 11) age phase will be those which:

- are within the grasp of a 5- to 11-year-old child
- are relevant to events and the children's experiences
- lend themselves to testing by the children.

As an effective teacher of primary science, you will need to have knowledge of:

- the content of statutory and non-statutory curricula and frameworks
- the nature of science
- key ideas in science
- key ideas in science subject pedagogy
- strengths and areas for development in your personal knowledge and understanding (through an audit of subject knowledge) and in your teaching of science (through 'needs analysis' exercises or professional development reviews).

What can you do to support the acquisition and development of this knowledge?

- observe good practice
- network with other teachers and schools
- contact international and national organizations and draw upon the expertise, resources, professional development they offer (for example, the Association for Science Education, or Science Learning Centres)
- continue to read, discuss, challenge and question.

Conclusion

In this chapter we have discussed the principles underpinning primary science education, acknowledging the importance of forming a view of what science is, its nature and its development. The historical development of approaches to the teaching of science were also explored, related to theoretical frameworks which have influenced the ways in which we educate in science. General principles to guide teachers of science were outlined. All of these elements have shaped the practice of primary science education, discussed now in Chapter 8.

References

Adams, D. (1979), *The Hitchhikers Guide to the Galaxy*. London: Pan MacMillan.

Asoko, H. (2002), 'Developing conceptual understanding in primary science.' *Cambridge Journal of Education* 32 (2)

Barrett, N. (2006), 'Creative Partnerships: Manchester and Salford.' www.ioe.mmu.ac.uk/cue/seminars/BARRETT%20Urban%20seminar1.doc (Accessed July 2007.)

Claxton, G. (1991), *Educating the Inquiring Mind*. London: Harvester Wheatsheaf.

Department for Education and Employment (DfEE)/ Qualifications and Curriculum Authority (QCA) (1999), *The National Curriculum for England*. London: HMSO.

Department for Education and Skills (DfES) (2002), *Key Stage 3 National Strategy. Framework for Teaching Science: Years 7, 8 and 9*. London: DfES Publications.

Department for Education and Skills (DfES) (2004), *Every Child Matters: Change for Children*. Nottingham: DfES Publications.

Department of Education Northern Ireland (2007), *The Education (Curriculum Minimum Content) Order (Northern Ireland) 2007*. London: The Stationery Office.

Donaldson, M. (1978), *Children's Minds*. London: Fontana.

Fensham, P. (1992), 'Science and Technology' in P.W. Jackson (ed.), *Handbook of Research on Curriculum*. New York: Macmillan.

Goodwin, A. (1994), 'Wonder and the teaching of science.' *Education in Science* 159, 8–9.

Harlen, W. (2006a), *Teaching, Learning and Assessing Science 5–12* (4th edition). London: SAGE.

Harlen, W. (ed.) (2006b), *ASE Guide to Primary Science Education*. Hatfield: Association for Science Education.

Harlen, W. and Qualter, A. (2004), *The Teaching of Science in Primary Schools*. London: David Fulton.

Hayes, D. (2006), *Inspiring Primary Teaching*. Exeter: Learning Matters.

Keogh, B. and Naylor, S. (1999), 'Concept Cartoons, teaching and learning in science: An evaluation.' *International Journal of Science Education* 21 (4), 431– 46.

Matthews, M.R. (2000), 'Constructivism in Science and Mathematics Education' in D.C. Phillips (ed.), *National Society for the Study of Education, 99th Yearbook*. Chicago: University of Chicago Press.

Medawar, P. (1967), *The Art of the Soluble*. Oxford: Oxford University Press.

Millar, R. and Osborne, J. (1998), *Beyond 2000: Science Education for the Future*. London: King's College London.

Office for Standards in Education/Her Majesty's Inspectorate (Ofsted/HMI) (2006), *The Annual Report of Her Majesty's Chief Inspector of Schools 2005/2006*. London: Ofsted.

Osborne, J. and Collins, S. (2002), in Duggan and Gott, (2002), 'What sort of science education do we really need?' *International Journal of Science Education* 24 (7), 30.

Osborne, R. and Freyberg, P. (1985), *Learning in Science: The Implications of Children's Science*. Auckland: Heinemann.

Parliamentary Office of Science and Technology (2003), *Postnote Primary Science*. London: Parliamentary Office of Science and Technology.

Peacock, G.A. (2000), *Teaching Science in Primary Schools: A Handbook of Lesson Plans, Knowledge and Teaching Methods*. London: Letts.

Qualifications and Curriculum Authority (1998), *A Scheme of Work for Key Stages One and Two: Science*. Middlesex: QCA Publications.

Qualifications and Curriculum Authority/Department for Education and Employment (1998), *Science: A Scheme of Work for Key Stages 1 and 2*. Middlesex: QCA Publications.

Random House (2006), *Unabridged Dictionary*. London: Random House.

Ratcliffe, M. and Grace, M. (2003), *Science Education for Citizenship: Teaching Socio-scientific Issues*. Maidenhead: Open University Press.

Ridley, M. (2006), 'Francis Crick: Discoverer of the Genetic Code.' *New Scientist,* 2576, 37– 45.

Roden, J. (2005), *Achieving QTS: Reflective Reader: Primary Science*. Exeter: Learning Matters.

Scottish Government: School Education (2006), *Curriculum for Excellence: Building the Curriculum*. Edinburgh: Scottish Government/Scottish Qualifications Authority.

Sharp, J. (ed.) (2004), *Developing Primary Science*. Exeter: Learning Matters.

SPACE Research Report (1991) *Evaporation and Condensation*. Liverpool: Liverpool University Press.

Stenhouse, D. (1985), *Active Philosophy in Education and Science*. London: George Allen & Unwin.

Teachernet, 'Common errors children make and misconceptions they often have in science.' Supply teaching/study materials. www.teachernet.gov.uk/supply teaching/ (Accessed June 2007.)

Training and Development Agency (TDA) (2007), *Professional Standards for Qualified Teacher Status*. London: TDA for Schools.

Vygotsky, L. S. (1978), *Mind in Society: The Development of Higher Psychological Processes*. M. Colt, V. John-Steiner, S. Scribner and E. Souberman (eds and trans). Cambridge, MA: Harvard University Press. (Original work published in 1934.)

Wallace, B. (2002), *Teaching Thinking Skills Across the Early Years*. London: David Fulton.

Wolpert, L. (1992), 'Why it's all Greek.' *Guardian*, 29 October.

Teaching Science: The Practice

8

Kate Blacklock and Debbie Eccles

Chapter Outline

A discussion between three 7-year-old children and their teacher.

Teacher: What is an experiment?

Child 1: Where you learn stuff.

Child 2: You're finding things out for yourself.

Child 3: You make things when you do experiments.

Child 2: Like circuits.

Child 1: And puppets.

Child 3: No, that's design technology.

Introduction

In Chapter 7 we discussed the principles underpinning science education. In this chapter we explore turning those principles into effective practice. At the heart of this discussion will be the 'Planning–Teaching–Assessing' cycle, which drives practice. However, the divisions between these three elements or stages of practice are artificial, since all are interdependent and intermingled: planning changes as teaching happens; assessment is ongoing; and so on. Therefore, issues addressed in the first section of the chapter on 'planning' apply to teaching and assessing also. In singling out what teachers know in order to plan effectively for science learning, it is implicit that this same bank of knowledge will be what drives teaching and assessing: the divisions are arbitrary.

Planning

The lesson plan is a product. It is the *process* of planning that decides whether or not that lesson plan will bring to life an element of learning for the children, whether or not it will motivate and inspire, whether or not it will enable the children to learn. Overemphasis on the mechanics of lesson planning can militate against effective teaching. So, for example, the teacher who rigidly adheres to a proforma for planning, filling in boxes with two learning objectives, two assessment outcomes, a resource list, a timed sequence of activities and so on, may be in danger of losing sight of the rationale – the 'why?' and the 'how?'. The thought processes underpinning the most effective planning are not easily caught on paper, but will be immediately obvious in observing the practice, since this teacher will have drawn on knowledge of the children, knowledge of the subject and the curriculum, and knowledge of teaching and learning in order to anticipate questions, to challenge, to vary the pace, to involve the children and to meet needs. He or she will also be able to adapt at a moment's notice to an unexpected opportunity or event. A tall order indeed!

The elements underpinning planning will be discussed in further detail here. The order does not reflect significance or priority, since all are essential.

Knowledge of curriculum

Planning for science will of course be based on programmes of study for statutory curricula and on schemes of work arising from those programmes of study. How many teachers have read the introductions to these documents, which show the principles that have formed the statutory content and give a flavour of the values and beliefs, aims and purposes which drive the curriculum? It is not immediately apparent from the content headings of the National Curriculum for Science in England that 'Scientific method… is a spur to critical and creative thought', and that children should 'recognise the cultural significance of science and trace its worldwide development' (DfEE/QCA, 1999: 76). As Professor John White pointed out in relation to the changes introduced by the review of the National Curriculum in 1999, and more specifically, to the inclusion of aims:

> Although these aims were presented simply as a list, without any rationale, they are an interesting development. They place a good deal of emphasis on the pupil's personal well-being, practical reasoning and preparation for civic life. Sixty per cent of the items in the list are about the personal qualities we would like pupils to have. (White, 2005: 4)

The breadth of the curriculum is best represented here, away from the minutiae of content specifications. We urge you to engage with the introductions to your curricula and consider the extent to which they are reflected in your planning and implementation.

Having ensured familiarity with aims and broader purposes, the balance between different areas of the science curriculum needs to be considered. Do each of the programmes of study and associated attainment targets have equal weighting? Successive government departments have proved reluctant to specify and legislate for the proportion of time to be devoted to particular parts of the science curriculum, thinking here primarily about the balance (or perhaps lack of balance) between scientific enquiry and the concept-based programmes of study. Perhaps this is positive, with too much prescription already existing. Science education researchers and educators have long recognized that the two aspects to science go hand-in-glove. On the one hand, there are the process skills and attitudes which are involved in scientific enquiry; on the other, the body of knowledge – or concepts – of science. You cannot have one without the other. We know that learning the concepts happens most effectively through applying the skills of scientific enquiry but equally, these skills cannot be acquired in a vacuum. They are developed and honed in learning concepts and by progressing in understanding of these concepts.

Scientific enquiry has been neglected in primary science education (see Chapter 7). There is possibly no faster way to effect changes in practice in schools than to change the emphasis in national tests. This is precisely what happened in England. The national assessment tests have included increasing numbers of questions on or about scientific enquiry. It had to feature more prominently in schools' planning, teaching and assessing if they were to maintain levels of achievement in national tests.

Remember that national curricula usually express a *minimum* entitlement. This is the case in England: the statutory content is the minimum that must be provided, and thus planning need not exclude topics or concepts simply because the curriculum does not specify their coverage. (This relates to the issue of whether to introduce the particle model to primary aged children, as discussed in Chapter 7.) It should also reflect life 'beyond the curriculum', drawing on the experiences, expertise and environment of the school's community.

Knowledge of the subject

How much knowledge of the subject do you need in order to teach effectively? This is a complex question, because undoubtedly with knowledge comes increased confidence. However, you should revisit the messages in Chapter 7 in order to formulate your own response to the question. We discussed the transience of knowledge in science, and suggested that knowledge of the *nature* of the subject and of its development was far more important than knowledge of the content. It is certainly true that 'the more you know, the more you know there's still to know'! Audits of your subject knowledge are helpful (and necessary in order to take charge of your own professional development in science), and there are resources available to support you in this. Again as referred to in the previous chapter, Professional Standards for Teachers in England (Training and Development Agency, 2007) are less specific than previous versions about the content knowledge, and give scope to place emphasis, rightly, on demonstrating your knowledge of the children and of how to teach science effectively.

Knowledge of children and of children's learning

Chapter 7 explored theories of learning that have shaped our approaches to science education today. There is strong support for applying constructivist principles to primary science education. For the reasons previously explained, it is important that you reflect on these principles, evaluating them in relation to your own practice.

All of our accumulated knowledge about *how* children learn science confirms that it is certainly not a straight line progression, ever onwards and upwards. A powerful image is the U-shaped learning curve (Spink, 2002), which is not only applicable to learning science. It is ubiquitous in discussions of language acquisition, psychology, business systems, medicine and many others.

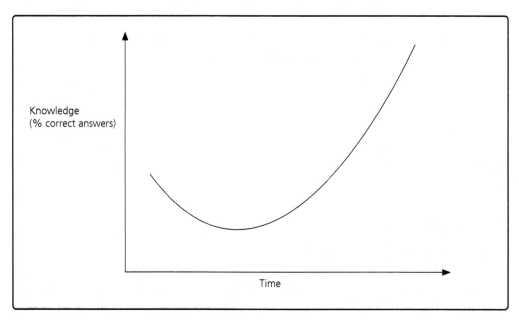

Figure 8.1 The U-shaped learning curve

What this suggests is that for learning to progress, we have to go through the 'trough of uncertainty' (the 'dip' in the curve) where we appear to know less than we did before. This arises when our existing ideas and concepts are challenged. We are questioning what we thought we already knew and trying to apply knowledge to new situations, probably having to adapt or change it as we do so.

At a superficial level, it means that if I, as a teacher, send learners away more confused than when I began to teach them, then surely I have succeeded, as I have progressed their learning into the next part of the curve, the trough! Of course, this is not satisfactory – my responsibility as a teacher is to enable learners to move through the period of uncertainty. The model does however sit comfortably with constructivist views: it acknowledges that learners will already have ideas (and we know from the research detailed in Chapter 7 that many of these ideas will be misconceptions); that the ideas need to be questioned and interrogated; and that the teacher needs to provide opportunities for children to test out existing ideas, to assess others' ideas, and to apply new ideas.

Your planning should both generate the knowledge of the children (and their ideas) and draw upon that knowledge. It will include the planning of differentiated work; of means for finding out children's ideas; and of suitable activities to develop these ideas. Success in this will be exemplified by your responding to pupils' diverse learning needs; overcoming potential barriers to learning and assessment for individuals and groups of pupils; and the resultant setting of suitable learning challenges.

Knowledge of how to teach science

Pedagogical Content Knowledge (PCK) concerns the ways in which a teacher *translates* the three areas of knowledge discussed here (of the subject, of the curriculum and of the children's learning) into their teaching practice.

You will draw on your knowledge of common pupil misconceptions such as 'air has no weight', your knowledge of curriculum requirements (for example 'to recognize differences between solids, liquids and gases'), and your knowledge of the children's prior experiences and learning needs to plan appropriate teaching strategies and activities. (In the example above, this might include the children exploring what happens when an inflated balloon and an un-inflated balloon are suspended from each end of a balance.)

Planning for scientific enquiry

This has been singled out for attention here, given what we know of the relative neglect of scientific enquiry and also because of its proven positive effects on children's learning and attainment in science. Scientific enquiry should be at the heart of science work undertaken by children in the primary years, and this message is overt in the Science National Curriculum for England (DfEE/QCA, 1999). The 'breadth of study' for each Key Stage reinforces the teaching of knowledge, skills and understanding through science investigations, familiar contexts, looking at the role of science in society, and communicating ideas.

Some teachers point to the 'absence' of units on Scientific Enquiry in the QCA Scheme of Work (QCA/DfEE, 1998): the following can be a telling activity.

Pause to think

With a colleague, select three units from the QCA Scheme of Work for Science and analyse the individual learning objectives:

- How many of these learning objectives are Scientific Enquiry (Sc1) objectives?
- How many are objectives relating to Life Processes and Living Things (Sc2), Materials and their Properties (Sc3) and Physical Processes (Sc4)?

Scientific enquiry *is* embedded in this scheme.

To plan effectively for scientific enquiry, you need to be very familiar with its content and breadth – information you gain from your programmes of study and schemes of work. However, it is necessary to ensure that key elements are not being overlooked or key messages undelivered. For example, the programme of study for scientific enquiry in the National Curriculum for England divides into two strands: the 'Investigative skills' strand, familiar to all teachers; and the perhaps less familiar 'Ideas and Evidence' strand – less familiar because it rarely seems to feature in schools' schemes of work or explicitly in teachers' planning. This strand is where children can learn to value the *nature* of science. It can potentially do more than any other part of the science curriculum to militate against the pervasive view that 'science is about right answers'. Its emphasis is on creative thinking; the 'stories' behind scientific developments; the tentative nature of scientific ideas; and on how science proceeds through the gathering of evidence and testing of ideas.

The other strand, 'Investigative skills' is presented in a linear way: Planning; Obtaining and Presenting Evidence; and Considering Evidence and Evaluating. But again, we would encourage you to conceptualize this as a cycle.

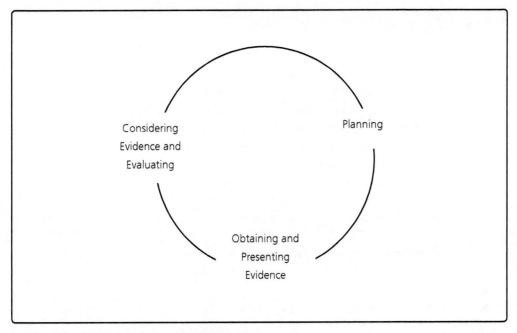

Figure 8.2 The cycle of investigative skills

This better represents the process of scientific enquiry, when the outcome of asking a question or investigating an idea is usually a further question or a different idea which also needs investigating – a journey without end!

Children need to go through this cycle for themselves, and so your planning must address how you will enable the children to learn how to plan and how you will ensure they have time to learn skills of considering evidence and evaluating outcomes.

Planning for effective questioning

Planning must also incorporate the effective use of questioning to enhance learning. The following, produced by the authors and Charlotte Clarke, and the result of working with teachers in Blackpool, provides a guide for evaluating your planning for questioning and the extent to which you promote questions and questioning among the children.

Pause to think

- When are questions used to elicit pupils' understanding?
- How effective are questions used in plenary sessions?
- Are appropriate teacher questions recorded in planning?
- Are questions closed (requiring a specific response or 'right' answer) or open (for example, 'What do *you* think?')?
- Is a range of question types used (such as comparison questions; action/problem-solving questions; measurement questions)?
- Are pupils invited to raise questions of their own? How?
- How frequently are pupils asked to generate their own questions?
- When pupils ask questions are they, or other pupils, given the opportunity to answer them?
- Are effective questions an integral part of science displays?
- Do pupils have a book, display area or post-box where they can log their science questions?
- Are pupils given adequate thinking time before a response to a question is required?

Levels of planning

Long-term planning for science

This will provide an overview of a whole year's work, and should be placed in the context of the whole school's scheme so that the work it contains is age and ability appropriate, and meets the requirements of the National Curriculum. The long-term plan sets the sequence of work and is vital for ensuring continuity and progression (that is, that the children will build on what has gone before in a planned way – continuity – and that they will progress in their understanding, knowledge and skills – progression). The plan will also enable links between topics and across subject areas to be identified.

The following figure provides a model for long-term planning, and was constructed by a regional science advisory team.

Year	Autumn		Spring		Summer	
Year 1 (Lower KS1)	**Ourselves** How many cubes/lolly sticks can you pick up? What happens when we exercise?	**Light** What colours can be seen best in dim light?	**Forces** Which is the best car? Where is it easiest to use a sit-on-toy?	**Materials** Which is the best material for mopping up?	**Living Things in Their Environment** What colour mini-beasts live where?	
Year 2 (Upper KS1)	**Living Things and Plant Life** What happens to plants kept in the dark/not watered?	**Electricity** Which legs are connected to which in the wires spider?	**Sound** How can we make the best ear muffs/quiet hat?	**Health and Growing up** Whose baby is this?	**Materials – Changing** Where is the best place for Jack Frost to live? How can we make the best cakes? How can we make the jelly dissolve?	
Year 3 (Lower KS2)	**Ourselves – Moving Seeing and Hearing** Are two eyes better than one? Are two ears better than one?	**Materials – Properties** Which is the best paper? Which is the best carrier bag? Which fabric makes the best tea cosy?	**Plants** How can we grow the best plant?	**Forces** How can we make the best helicopter? How can we change the car to make it go faster?		
Year 4 (Lower KS2)	**Rocks and soils** Which is the best filter paper?	**Electricity** How can we make the best switch?	**Ourselves – Eating and Staying Healthy** What do different liquids do to our teeth?	**Materials – Mixing, Separating and Changing** Do all substances dissolve?	**Living Things in Their Environment** What do snails like to eat? Where do woodlice like to live?	
Year 5 (Upper KS2)	**Light** Which materials are best for shadow puppets? How can we make the biggest shadow?	**Sound** How can we change pitch?	**Forces** How can we make the best parachute?	**Earth in Space** What happens to shadows through the day? How can we make the biggest craters?	**Materials – Water Cycle** What affects evaporation? How much will dissolve?	**Living Things in Their Environment** How do dandelions differ?
Year 6 (Upper KS2)	**Our Bodies and Healthy Living** What happens to our pulse rate when we exercise? Where do things rot the best?	**Electricity** How can we alter the brightness of a bulb?	**Plants and Life Cycles** What effect does temperature have on plant growth (N.B. not germination)?	**Materials – Solids, Liquids and Gases** How can we make the dried fruit rise more quickly?	Transition topics	

Figure 8.3 A model for long-term planning

The plan addresses the ratio of scientific enquiry to knowledge-focused activities carefully, containing at least 50 per cent of enquiry-based work at Key Stage 1 and at least 40 per cent at Key Stage 2.

Medium-term planning for science

This takes the topic or unit areas from the long-term plan and specifies the next layer of detail – that is, the learning objectives linked to appropriate activities and the learning outcomes – so that both children and teachers know what are the success criteria. Objectives and outcomes need to be expressed clearly and precisely at this stage of planning. Objectives must not simply *describe* what the children will do, they must focus on what the children will have the opportunity to *learn*. So, 'to make shapes with plasticine' is not a valid objective because it describes the activity, not the learning.

The example of a medium-term plan shown in the following figure was adapted by a school from the QCA Scheme of Work, Unit 2E (QCA/DfEE, 1999)

LEARNING OBJECTIVES CHILDREN SHOULD LEARN	TEACHING ACTIVITIES and KEY VOCABULARY	LEARNING OUTCOMES CHILDREN WILL
that sometimes pushes and pulls change the shape of objects	Children explore how to make a variety of shapes *eg sausage, ball, worm*, with plasticine describe what action they used *eg twist, stretch*. and Classify the action as a push or a pull. Record as drawings with labels *Key vocabulary: push, pull, twist, stretch, squeeze*	describe what they did using words such as *twist, squeeze, stretch, pull out* and classify actions as pushes or pulls *eg stretching is a pull, squeezing is a push*
that pushes or pulls can make things speed up or slow down or change direction	With a collection of toy cars, children decide how to make them move faster, slower, or change direction. Record work in pictures and tables with simple explanations. • *Key vocabulary: speed up, slow down, fast, fastest, faster, slow, slower, slowest, surface, friction, slide, smooth, rough, heavy, change direction, turn, throw, stop.*	describe how to make things speed up or change direction *eg by saying when I push the car hard it goes faster and faster, when I hit the ball it went off to the side*

(adapted from QCA/DfEE, 1999)

Figure 8.4 Model for a medium-term plan

This school has adapted the activities given in the QCA scheme while still applying the learning objectives and outcomes. They are aware that the national scheme suggests *possible* teaching activities only and that, in many cases, their teachers and children generate activities that are more innovative, creative and effective at meeting the stated objectives.

Short-term planning in science

A short-term plan contains a set of activities for a week, a day or a lesson, and is based on the needs of the children. Teachers use short-term plans to devise the structure and content of each lesson/session and to plan the specific details, such as key questions, resources, differentiation and the 'what, when and how?' of assessment. The plan may take the form of an annotated medium-term plan, a proforma adopted by the school, or a re-working of a plan extracted from a book or downloaded from the internet. An important word here is 're-working': for a plan to be implemented successfully, the teacher has to have engaged with it and made it his or her own. As suggested in the introduction to this section, it is the process of planning that is most important, rather than the content.

With all of these plans in place for primary science, where is the scope for 'seizing the moment'? The irony is that planning thoroughly gives teachers the confidence to be flexible and spontaneous. Alison (see case study below) is a highly skilled teacher, renowned for her thorough planning and organization, who is nevertheless able to make full use of the rich potential of the unexpected.

Case study

Alison is the teacher of a Reception class (4- and 5-year-old children). She had planned an afternoon of P.E. (developing skills in throwing and rolling games with bean bags and balls), then a return to the week's sequence of group activities. It began to hail. She quickly gathered the children by a large window so that all 25 of them (including herself) could reach outside to feel the hail falling on their hands. They watched it bounce on the ground, they caught it and described it, they made it melt, they listened to the sounds it made hitting the metal window frames and the flat roof of their classroom. This prompted Alison to fetch metal trays. They held these outside and listened again to the sounds made. Immediately afterwards, the children were given the opportunity to re-create the 'hail music' with musical instruments.

(Adapted from Spink, E. in Basford and Hodson, 2008)

Planning for assessment

Most of the science assessment you plan for on a day-to-day basis will be assessment for learning. You will plan questions or activities which will inform you of the children's progress in relation to learning objectives, or which will reveal existing ideas and also inform the children of developments in their learning. A key factor to consider is the frequency with which opportunities for assessing elements of learning in science will occur. Particular science concepts associated with topic areas (the knowledge statements of the programmes of study) may only feature two or three times over the course of a child's primary education. For example, the concepts of 'forces' are not taught on a weekly or even termly basis. Learning objectives related to these areas must be assessed as and when they happen. On the other hand, for science process objectives, the component skills are ongoing in application, and there will be many more opportunities to assess them. It is far more effective to focus your assessment observations on a small number of children at a time and for the duration of an activity, rather than to attempt to assess all children against all objectives simultaneously.

Strategies for teaching science

Many of the teaching strategies already discussed in this book will apply equally well to the teaching of science. It would be worthwhile for you to make a note of these strategies and evaluate the extent to which they will support your science teaching. What we will do here is focus on a smaller number of strategies which have particular relevance for science education.

Strategies to enhance the science teaching environment

The 'learning environment' is a complex notion to consider. At its broadest, we are considering the physical, the social and the emotional environment offered to learners, ensuring the classroom is a place where both the children and the teachers want to be and where they can be successful.

To best support learning in science the physical environment should be interactive and encourage autonomy. To learn to enquire scientifically, the children must be able to plan what they need to do and what they need to use. Science practical equipment should be readily available and clearly labelled, but with the option for children to choose the appropriate resources.

Science learning relies upon interactions occurring between children and between adults and children. The significance of interaction can be reflected in the way you choose to organize the physical space for science, or in the nature and quality of displays. The most effective science displays echo the kinds of interactions and discussions that drive science lessons: for example, by posing questions, by setting challenges with moveable pieces ('Can you place these forces arrows to show the direction of the force?'), by creating spaces where children can share information or post snippets on things that have caught their attention, by offering games or puzzles ('What's in this bag?'). A carefully crafted and artistically presented display may be eye-catching, but it has made no contribution to learning if the children do not use it or understand what it is about.

The social and emotional environment created may vary with the type of science lesson being carried out: investigations often require group work; research from secondary sources might be conducted in pairs; initial discussion of ideas may take place across the whole class. But the type of culture you create is vital for effective science learning: it must be one which is open to new ideas; which values any and all contributions; which questions and wonders and tests out. The question of 'which method of grouping is best for science?' is one of the most difficult to answer. It will be determined by your knowledge of the children and the context, and by your experience in teaching. However, be wary of 'ability groups' unless you have carefully explored the meaning of this question – ability in *what*? Many ability groups are based on the children's performance or achievement in English and/or mathematics. Does this have any relevance to likely ability in science? Children who have less developed literacy skills may shine in science lessons where their ideas are heard and valued (and not necessarily written down). 'Mixed ability' groups can be highly successful in science, as those with ideas which more closely relate to the scientifically accepted idea (not necessarily the 'more able' child) can help to scaffold the learning of their peers.

It is important to monitor the roles undertaken by individuals when working within a group – and to intervene appropriately. The commendable motive of encouraging groups to 'manage' themselves independently of the teacher is to be questioned if the children are always able to self-select roles within their groups. You will already have noticed the 'doers', those children always keen to have hands-on involvement as quickly as possible; the scribes, who record investigations; the leaders; and the resource-gatherers. To ensure each child has access to the full range of science process skills, their habitual roles must be rotated through your intervention. The doers have an entitlement to learn to record and communicate science; the scribes have an entitlement to improve their skill in measuring; and so on.

The learning environment for science should be sensitive to the needs of all the children, culturally, morally, socially and intellectually. If children are involved in forming this environment and in taking decisions on its development then they are more likely to engage with the learning that takes place there.

Strategies to support science teaching

Chapter 7 proposed that the constructivist framework effectively supports learning in science; and successful teaching strategies will be those that enable this framework to operate. Since learners' ideas are central to constructivist learning, strategies that enable children to articulate their ideas and discuss them with others are vital. The SPACE research project (1991) used the following techniques to elicit children's ideas:

- structured writing or drawing
- completing a picture
- individual discussion
- compiling log books (over a longer period of time than the above).

Many other techniques have been described in primary science education literature (such as concept cartoon, concept maps and peer interviews). However, if our primary goal is to enable children to articulate their thoughts, the first priority has to be to create and offer sufficient time to think. The 'think–pair–share' technique can do this, and elicit ideas, very effectively.

Example Think–Pair–Share in practice

The teacher has shown the children a short extract from the film of *The Iron Giant* (Warner Brothers, 1999, based on *The Iron Man* by Ted Hughes). These are the instructions which followed.

Think: 'How many sources of light did you notice? What were they?'
           (Individual thinking time of up to one minute.)

Pair: 'Talk about the sources of light with your partner. Did they spot any different ones?'
           (Paired thinking and discussion time for up to three minutes. The teacher monitors several discussions to identify some of the ideas emerging.)

Share: 'So, what sources of light did we see?'
           (The teacher invites one pair initially to share their thoughts and then invites the other pairs to expand upon the original list, noting misconceptions and secure concepts.)

Gaining access to children's ideas and prior knowledge not only guides your planning of the next steps but also enables more effective differentiation (the allocating of tasks with varying degrees of challenge to different children).

Using a 'KWL grid' (Know; Want to know; Learned) can be useful in this (see Figure 8.5), as the children specify what it is they want to know about a certain topic, and objectives can follow from there.

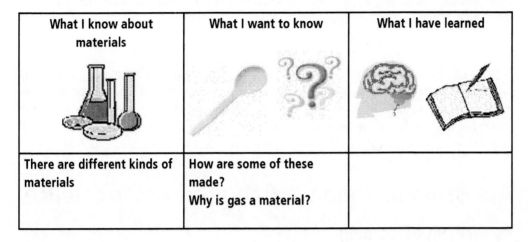

What I know about materials	What I want to know	What I have learned
There are different kinds of materials	How are some of these made? Why is gas a material?	

Figure 8.5 The KWL grid

The next steps in a constructivist teaching approach, arising from the SPACE research and discussed by Watt (1998), include (adapted from Watt) in Sherrington, 1998):

- building on children's ideas through investigation, and providing opportunities for children to test their ideas
- testing the 'right' idea alongside the children's ideas
- making imperceptible changes perceptible (for example, 'capturing' water vapour from a kettle and condensing it on a cold metal tray)
- helping children to generalize between contexts
- refining children's use of vocabulary (for example, enabling them to learn that 'dissolving' and 'melting' cannot be used interchangeably and that a table is not a table when it is a science table!).

Teaching through analogy is a further strategy common to primary science. Many of the ideas in science are abstract, and this can make them difficult to engage with. 'Energy' is a good example. It is an extremely useful explanatory concept and is one of the basic ideas at the heart of all scientific knowledge and understanding: but it is a wholly abstract concept. And so we use analogies (and similes, metaphors, models and representations) to convey the meaning of abstract ideas and processes:

> The aim of analogy is to encourage learners to take elements from a situation that they
> have experience and knowledge of and to transfer those attributes to the new situation
> they are trying to understand. (Parker, 2004: 30)

Asoko and de Boo (2001) provide a rich source of analogies that can very effectively
support children's learning in science. However, as they also would acknowledge, analogies
must be applied with caution. They all have limitations and all reach the point where they
no longer adequately convey the intended meaning. If you, as the teacher, are not sure of
where the analogy begins to break down, there is a risk that it will foster misconceptions.

Assessing and monitoring progress in science

Assessment of learning

Assessment of learning, or summative assessment, provides a summary of attainment at a
particular point, such as at the end of a unit, the end of a term or the end of a school year. It
can only provide a 'snapshot' of attainment in science at that time. Assessment of learning in
science usually takes the form of written or drawn responses to specific tasks and questions.
It will be used for the following purposes:

- to provide evidence of achievement for the school's self-evaluation data
- to facilitate long-term planning
- to aid progression through end-of-year assessments for the following teacher
- to report to parents
- to celebrate the achievement of children.

Assessment of learning involves making judgements according to the standards or levels
of attainment against which all children's attainment is measured. In England, this will take
place with reference to the level descriptions for the four attainment targets.

When assessing children in your class, you may find it useful (and indeed it may be
school practice) to compile portfolios of children's work in science, summatively assessed
and levelled. The most effective way to achieve clarity and consensus in summative
assessment is through whole staff collaboration. Pieces of work are discussed by groups of
colleagues and a consensus reached as to the level and achievements of the child. Portfolios
so compiled will provide a useful benchmark for subsequent assessment of learning in
science. Examples of assessments of children's work, and applications of level descriptions,
are available from the QCA's website (www.qca.org.uk).

Assessment for learning

Assessment for learning (or formative assessment) in science is essential if children are to build on their current thinking and make continued progress in developing their skills and knowledge and understanding of the world and its phenomena:

> Assessment is one of the most powerful educational tools for promoting effective learning. But it must be used in the right way. There is no evidence that increasing the amount of testing will enhance learning. Instead the focus needs to be on helping teachers use assessment as part of teaching and learning, in ways that will raise pupils' achievement. (Black and Wiliam, 1998)

Assessment for learning involves children in their learning, and should facilitate the tailoring of the curriculum to fit their individual needs. Strategies for enabling children to become involved in assessment for learning include:

- finding out what children know about the planned topic
- involving children in choosing appropriate learning objectives and success criteria (so they will learn how to recognize when they have been successful)
- planning objectives in child-friendly (that is, child-accessible) language
- encouraging a climate rich in questioning, discussion, dialogue and listening
- involving children regularly in self-assessment, with sufficient time planned for ensuring that children know what they need to do to achieve success and for reviewing work
- giving thought and time to the planning and implementation of peer assessment
- target-setting with the children.

Unrealistic target-setting can be highly demotivating and instil, if one set of targets is rapidly followed by another, a view that 'the teacher is never satisfied'. Wherever possible, the teacher and the child should agree on the target. Some targets may need to be set more than once. For example, children might need ongoing reinforcement of the target of making predictions based on scientific knowledge. Figure 8.6 contains a set of layered targets for scientific enquiry in Key Stages 1 and 2, developed by teachers in Lancashire.

My Targets and Achievements in Scientific Enquiry

I can:

- Start to understand the importance of information from other sources
- Have an idea about what might happen
- Describe what I see
- Use non-standard measures
- Talk about work i.e. things that are familiar – it's red, it's cold
- Draw pictures and simple charts e.g. pictograms about my work
- Ask questions using words such as how? And why?

My Targets and Achievements in Scientific Enquiry

I can:

- Use simple texts to find information
- Suggest ways to find out more about things I want to know
- Use simple equipment with non-standard measures to help me
- Use equipment and make observations
- Suggest how to make a test fair with support
- Describe observations and say whether I expected them
- Compare objects/living things/things that happen (three or more things)
- Record what I see on simple tables or charts e.g. prepare two column table, bar chart
- Make simple comparisons (three things), order results
- Use my senses to find out about things
- Ask questions such as 'what will happen if?'
- Understand some scientific vocabulary.

My Targets and Achievements in Scientific Enquiry

I can:

- Use simple texts to find information
- Suggest how my ideas might be tested and start to decide what observations and measurements I will need
- Measure length and mass using simple equipment with standard measures e.g. metre sticks, measuring jugs, balances, timers, thermometers
- Predict what I think will happen in an experiment
- With help carry out a fair test and explain why it is fair/recognize when a test is fair or unfair
- Compare three or more things
- Record the results of my tests or experiments in a variety of ways including tables/charts/using the computer
- Explain simple patterns from measurements taken
- Say what I have found out from my work

Figure 8.6 'My targets and achievements in scientific enquiry'

- Use some scientific vocabulary to explain my thoughts
- Understand the need to improve my work and make suggestions how to do this.

My Targets and Achievements in Scientific Enquiry

I can:

- Choose information to help me, from different sources provided, including the computer
- Make the most of the planning decisions when planning an investigation
- Show I know why fair tests are needed and know how to vary one factor whilst keeping other factors the same
- Make predictions about what is going to happen in a test
- Select appropriate equipment from a range of equipment
- Use equipment effectively, reading standard measures
- Make a series of observations, comparing five or more things
- Sometimes take repeated readings
- Present my results clearly using tables and bar charts, take repeated recordings and discuss my ideas
- Plot points to make a line graph and notice how these can show patterns in my data
- Take account of these patterns when drawing conclusions to the science that I know
- Use scientific vocabulary with understanding
- Suggest improvements in my work and give reasons for what I say.

My Targets and Achievements in Scientific Enquiry

I can:

- Talk about cause and effect and some prominent scientists (e.g. Jenner)
- Choose information about books, articles, facts and CD-ROMs to help me find out answers to my questions
- Make all of the planning decisions when planning investigations
- Make predictions based on scientific knowledge and understanding
- Identify confidently the factors to be controlled or varied in a test
- Compare five or more things
- Select apparatus for a range of tasks and use it with care
- Measure with precision, safety and skill
- Repeat measurements and offer simple explanations for differences between measurements
- Record my results in a systematic way and present data as line graphs
- Draw conclusions which are consistent with the evidence and relate them to my scientific knowledge and understanding
- Use precise scientific vocabulary.

Figure 8.6 (continued)

Effective assessment for learning in science will lie at the heart of the practice of the most successful teacher of science: it drives the cycle of planning, teaching and assessing.

Conclusion

To teach science effectively you will draw upon an impressive range of knowledge, skills and understanding – most of which you already have in place! The discussion here has encouraged you to think carefully about the rationale underpinning your choices of approaches and techniques for planning, teaching and assessing science, to ensure that the decisions taken are pedagogically sound. You will also be drawing on your knowledge of the principles at the heart of effective science education. In the next chapter we leave behind the pragmatics of delivering a curriculum to primary-aged children, and focus on wider opportunities and challenges.

References

Asoko, H. and de Boo, M. (2001), *Analogies and Illustrations: Representing Ideas in Primary Science*. Hatfield: The Association for Science Education.

Black, P. and Wiliam, D. (1998), *Beyond the Black Box*. London: Kings College.

Department for Education and Employment (DfEE)/ Qualifications and Curriculum Authority (QCA) (1999), *The National Curriculum for England*. London: HMSO.

Parker, J. (2004), 'Knowledge and Understanding' in J. Sharp (ed.), *Developing Primary Science*. Exeter: Learning Matters.

Qualifications and Curriculum Authority/Department for Education and Employment (1998), *Science: A Scheme of Work for Key Stages 1 and 2*. Middlesex: QCA Publications.

Sherrington, R. (ed.) (1998), *ASE Guide to Primary Science Education*. Hatfield: ASE.

SPACE Research Project (1991) *SPACE Research Report*. Liverpool: Liverpool University Press.

Spink, E. (2002), 'Supporting Adult Learning' in M. Nolan (ed.), *Education and Support for Parenting*. Edinburgh: Harcourt Publishers.

Spink, E., Keogh, B. and Naylor, S. (2008) in Basford, J. and Hodson, E. (eds), *Teaching the Early Years Foundation Stage*. Exeter: Learning Matters.

Training and Development Agency (TDA) (2007), *Professional Standards for Qualified Teacher Status*. London: TDA for Schools.

Warner Brothers (1999), *The Iron Giant*. (DVD)

Watt, D. (1998), 'Children's learning of science concepts' in R. Sherrington (ed.), *ASE Guide to Primary Science Education*. Hatfield: The Association for Science Education.

White, J. (2005), *The Curriculum and the Child: The Selected Works of John White*. London: Routledge.

Teaching Science: Beyond the Curriculum

Kate Blacklock and Debbie Eccles

Chapter Outline

If you think there is only one answer, then you will only find one.
(Scottish Consultative Council on the Curriculum, 1996)

Introduction

The world, or rather, the universe, of science is so much bigger and grander than anything a statutory curriculum can encompass. The richness and diversity of science offers attractions and wonders for all learners and is best sampled through diverse approaches not limited to subject 'boxes'. This chapter will not discuss the mechanics of forging links between other curriculum subjects and science, since material already exists (and is constantly being produced) to support teachers in this. We take as a starting point the fact that the processes and approaches of science education are transferable across all curriculum areas and that teachers will seek to create and extend cross-curricular links that are meaningful and beneficial for their pupils.

What this chapter will do is offer opportunities for going beyond the boundaries of subject areas or current initiatives to explore overarching themes and dimensions in education, and the contribution the teaching and learning of science can make to them.

Science education and global citizenship

Education plays a vital role in helping children and young people recognise their responsibilities as citizens of the global community and it equips them with the skills required to make informed decisions and take responsible actions. (DFID, 2006)

If we were to place the word 'science' at the beginning of the above quote, it would be as valid and as strong a message: because science does have a particular part to play. Its role becomes even more apparent when considering the aims of a global dimension in teaching and the key concepts (as defined by the UK's Department for International Development, op cit).

The global dimension gives young people the opportunity to:

- critically examine their own values and attitudes
- appreciate the similarities between peoples everywhere, and value diversity
- understand the global context of their daily choices and local actions
- develop skills to help combat injustice, prejudice and discrimination.

The eight key concepts through which the global dimension can be understood are:

- global citizenship
- conflict resolution
- diversity
- human rights
- interdependence
- social justice
- sustainable development
- values and perceptions.

So, what contribution can our teaching of science make to developing these eight concepts? An issue that has been highlighted elsewhere in this book (and one which will be raised again later in this chapter) is the need to avoid tentative connections between subject areas/ topics if other connections would be more valid and meaningful. Yes, science can contribute to each of the above key concepts: but as an experienced teacher, I would not select science as the means to teach about conflict resolution or human rights specifically. These concepts will be implicit in my teaching of science (and perhaps conflict resolution will need to be explicit at some times!), but they will not feature in science objectives in lesson planning. This is not to say that study of the *breadth* of science, going beyond the curriculum, will not provide rich opportunities for these global concepts – of course it will. For example, when working with children on 'the human body' and considering specifically 'What is blood for?', the tale of Charles Drew never fails to rouse emotions and prompt discussion. Dr Charles Drew pioneered developments in blood transfusion by discovering a way of storing and separating blood. He set up the world's first blood bank. Charles spoke out about the racist practice of storing blood from white and black people separately. In 1950, he was fatally injured in a car crash but was turned away from the nearest hospital because he was black. Charles died before reaching the next hospital. (For further details see Feasey, 1999: 111, or www.scienceyear.com.)

We will now examine more closely specific contributions science can make to many of the global dimension key concepts.

Global citizenship

Knowledge, skills and understanding of concepts are necessary to become informed, active citizens. This notion links with the discussion in Chapter 7 of scientific literacy. Science education should seek to encourage learners to question, to seek evidence, and to wonder about the validity of so-called 'facts'. A useful way of promoting this with primary children can be to focus on advertisements, and ask: 'Where's the science?' Skin products advertisements can be a very rich source for this activity but there are numerous examples in all media of claims that ought to make informed citizens stop and think. Many, such as washing products, can be used in practical investigations (for example, testing stain removal, timing how long bubbles last for, comparing performance at different temperatures and so on). The children debate the claims made, questioning what they are told, looking for evidence, carrying out their own research based on the claims and then presenting their findings. This can occur in ways only limited by your and their imagination! Perhaps they will produce and film a television advertisement; carry out a web-link interview with a manufacturer; or design and market their own product.

Accepting the tentative nature of science is a vital part of developing questioning individuals, who we hope will become informed and active global citizens. With older primary children, the simple activity outlined below supports the notion well.

Pause to think

- Show two pieces of (seemingly identical) A4 size paper.
- Are they the same? Collect a list of the similarities.
- Is my piece of A4 paper the same size as yours?
- Everyone measures the length of their piece of paper and the results are gathered.
- There will be variation in the results, perhaps enormous variation if the children have used non-standard measures such as finger-width.
- The key question is *why* are there different results? How could we explain the differences? How do we know who is 'right'?
- The message is that even though there is supposed to be a 'right answer' (that is, a standardized size), we still cannot be positive and there is always immense scope for human (and equipment) error!

A classroom rich in discussion about the scientific issues surrounding us is making an enormous contribution to global citizenship. Primary-aged children will not be expected to deal with the science concepts underpinning global warming; but debate is raging about the issue, and this can and should be reflected in discussions with the children. A teacher should deal with questions from the children about scientific issues as they would a curriculum-based question (such as 'which materials dissolve?'): that is, in ways that lead to enquiry, investigation and learner involvement. For example: Teacher to the class – 'Kay has asked me whether I think global warming exists. What do you think? How can we find out more?' And later, following research appropriate to the children's ages and abilities: 'Does there seem to be more evidence in favour of global warming happening or against the idea? How do we decide what is "good" evidence? What do you think now?'

Global citizenship means looking beyond your immediate locality and seeing yourself as a citizen of the world. Geography topics help with this (for example, learning about similarities between my life and Puri's life in Kenya), and ICT has certainly opened up the world in ways which seemed impossible even ten years ago. For example, a primary school can have partner schools around the world with daily communication taking place. (If you do not currently have international contacts, liaise with your local Higher Education Initial Teacher Training institution, which is likely to have well-established international links that you can tap into.) However, science has an ideal area of learning for promoting global awareness – 'Earth and Space'. Anything that helps me to recognize the (relative) smallness of the Earth in the vastness of space (images from the Hubble space telescope or NASA's views of Earth from the moon are excellent resources) builds a sense of how special and precious our planet is, and makes it more likely that I can come to accept that people on the far side of the globe from me are as much my neighbours as people in my town, my country or my continent.

Diversity

Valuing diversity centres on understanding and respecting differences. Science and scientists are already wedded to this notion. Scientists are accepting and appreciative of differences, since there is potentially even more to learn from things or events that do not fit the expected patterns. The concept of diversity is present in the teaching of science content (for example, diversity in ourselves and in other living things), but is best developed through the teaching of the science process: the skills, attitudes and practices of scientific enquiry. Our science teaching must never reinforce stereotypes and must display emotional intelligence. In the box below, we ask you to consider the emotional intelligence exercised (or not) by the teacher whose classroom is described below.

Pause to think

What are the potential problems with a classroom display (in a class of 8- and 9-year-old children) labelled like this?

People in our class

The tallest is _____   The shortest is _____

The widest is _____   The heaviest is _____

This was an example from real life. A now 13-year-old girl from that class still recounts the day her picture was posted on the wall as the heaviest child. And yet the teacher had met her science objectives of 'to make observations and comparisons of relevant features'. This was learning about diversity without the essential accompaniment of respect for individuals.

Values and perceptions

Understanding global issues requires critical evaluation of different views and values and, of course, critical evaluation is crucial in scientific enquiry. However, the links between science education and 'values and perceptions' run deeper than this, because scientific enquiry requires the development of *attitudes* important to the furthering of science, as well as skills. In investigations within the primary classroom, we are encouraging attitudes of curiosity, perseverance, open-mindedness and critical reflection – and these are life skills, certainly not specific to science. They are attitudes that nurture global awareness.

Sustainable development

Sustainable development is an increasingly significant theme in education systems throughout the UK and other parts of the world. Teachers must have an understanding of its meaning, its guiding principles and its place within education.

Sustainable development is: 'development which meets the needs of the present without compromising the ability of future generations to meet their own needs' (www.sustainable-development.gov.uk).

The guiding principles are: living within environmental limits; ensuring a strong, healthy and just society; achieving a sustainable economy; using sound science responsibly; and promoting good governance (Teachernet). Science clearly plays a significant role in this, particularly since one of the principles asks us to 'use sound science responsibly'. Scientific enquiry and educating children to understand the nature of science involves developing an appreciation of what we may mean by *sound* science. and should expose children to well-chosen examples of responsible and irresponsible uses of science.

Priority areas for action in terms of sustainable development are:

- sustainable consumption and production
- climate change and energy
- natural resource protection and environmental enhancement
- sustainable communities.

These areas link directly with the science curriculum (for example, investigating energy transfers; learning about seasonal changes; identifying origins of materials; studying habitats; and inter-dependence), but also go beyond the science curriculum in ways which enrich learning more fundamentally. For example, 'environmental enhancement' does not feature in the National Curriculum for Science in England: and yet, as part of a cross-subject, 'beyond the curriculum' project, science skills and knowledge will undoubtedly grow.

As primary teachers, we must beware the temptation to focus too narrowly on 'recycling' as the main feature of sustainable development education. This is even more of a temptation in science, where recycling lends itself so well to learning about materials and their properties, sorting and classifying, and so on. As conveyed by the guiding principles, living within environmental limits (which includes *reducing* consumption, *reusing* and *recycling*) is just one element of sustainable development. Nevertheless, recycling *is* an important sustainable practice, and can make a significant contribution to the overarching theme within sustainability – changing behaviour:

Whilst 90% of people know that drinks cans can be recycled, only 50% say they've ever actually done it. (NOP World Research, 2004)

So your science lesson on sorting materials for recycling can help to bridge the theory-practice divide.

In the UK, government departments are attempting to embed sustainable development in education via a number of initiatives, including 'Healthy Schools'; school transport policies and travel plans; extended schools; curriculum reviews; and a 'Building Schools for the Future' programme. At school level, it requires whole school approaches to minimize the gaps between the stated values of the school and the values implicit in its actions, and to integrate the formal and non-formal curriculum. At classroom level, it involves you as a teacher – and a teacher of science – seeking purposeful connections between the learning of science principles and practice, and the development of sustainable practices. An excellent starting point can be conducting a sustainability survey using existing tools, such as the Eco-Schools Environmental Review Checklist (www.eco-schools.org.uk).

Pause to think

Make links between science education and the remaining key concepts, generating ideas for encouraging thinking about the global dimension and building it into the curriculum:

- conflict resolution
- human rights
- interdependence
- social justice.

By looking at science and its applications in social and global contexts, pupils are better prepared to take a positive and active place in tomorrow's world. (ASE, 2007: para 13)

Science education and creativity

Creativity and creative approaches to teaching and learning are at the forefront of current educational debate. The debate is not new, but the foundations of most recent education and curriculum revisions in England can be found in a document published in 1999: *All Our Futures: Creativity, Culture and Education* (National Advisory Committee on Creative and Cultural Education (NACCCE)). This report defined creativity (not a straightforward task), justified its importance in education and made recommendations for policies and practice. It made a very valuable distinction between teaching creatively and teaching for creativity (that is, teaching in ways which develop *children's* creative skills and potential).

Creative teaching will display characteristics of creative processes, and will also enable these processes to be engaged in and developed by the children. So, what are the characteristics of creative processes? NACCCE (op cit) described them thus: (they) always involve thinking or behaving imaginatively; this imaginative activity is purposeful; the processes generate something original; and the outcome must be of value in relation to the objective.

Measuring or testing for creativity is notoriously difficult. How would you fare in the test below?

Pause to think

- How many uses can you think of for a paperclip?
- After three minutes, compare and discuss your list with a colleague's.

Do you think the 'uses for a paperclip' task *is* assessing creativity? It (or similar) has been used extensively as a test for creativity in recruitment and selection processes. How valid and reliable would this measure be? You may wish to try something similar with the children you teach, perhaps substituting a paperclip with a cardboard roll – not as an assessment technique, of course, but as a means of encouraging the creative processes. Is it not the case that the true creative potential of the task is drawn out by the discussion that follows it, not by the scored items?

What role does science play in creativity in education? Science has a head start in teaching creatively and teaching for creativity because it *is* a creative subject. This may sound surprising to some, as the existence of an 'arts versus science' divide has been debated for decades, and the misconception that science is concerned with facts and the arts with the imagination is still prevalent. However, science is 'a distinctive form of creative human activity' (ASE, 2007: 1) and all that has been discussed in the preceding science chapters about the way science education should proceed promotes creativity: learner autonomy; discussion; valuing ideas; questioning; problem solving; investigating... all support the learning of science *and* the fostering of creativity. Babies and children are naturally creative and flexible in the ways in which they play and/or interact with the world, 'turning anything they can reach into something that they can investigate' (DCSF, 2007). Our teaching of science must foster this.

The following describes effective practice in relation to creativity and critical thinking according to England's Early Years Foundation Stage (op cit). However, it is fascinating to note how the guidance can be applied across the whole primary age range, and that a science focus overlays it so easily and productively. The points have been adapted from the original to emphasize connections with good practice in primary science education.

Effective practice in relation to creativity and critical thinking in primary science education

- Help children to make connections in their learning (e.g. role-play particles in materials changing state, see Chapter 7).
- Encourage creativity and opportunities for all children to link their ideas to new situations (as in the SPACE approach, see Chapter 7).
- Tell stories that present different possibilities within familiar situations (e.g. read *The Boy with Two Shadows* by Margaret Mahy).
- Value what parents tell you about the things their children do at home. Find out about the games, objects and stories that they particularly enjoy and build on these contexts.
- Provide opportunities for children to express their ideas in a variety of ways such as movement, dance, role play, painting (e.g. develop a role play of the story of Jenner developing a vaccine for smallpox, with different characters in the story putting forward different viewpoints: see www.bbc.co.uk/schools/famouspeople).
- Make it easier for children to make connections (and to express their ideas creatively) by giving them easy access to resources and materials.
- Provide resources from a variety of cultures.
- Create conditions within which children are inspired to be creative and rethink ideas (for example, create novel spaces by moving furniture or promote new relationships by changing groupings).
- Give children time to explore and develop their initiatives; encourage them to discuss what they are doing and what they want to achieve.

(Adapted from DCSF, 2007)

You, as a creative teacher, will be able to generate many more examples for the points in the list above. Science can support creative approaches, and science education can benefit enormously from increased creativity in learning and teaching. It will involve an element of risk-taking, in terms of trying new approaches and increasing the autonomy of the children: but the area just beyond our 'comfort zone' is where we all learn the most.

Science beyond the classroom

The following conversation took place between a 7-year-old child and her parent (a scientist):

> Child: Not everything's science you know, Mum.
>
> Parent: Oh yes it is.
>
> Child: No, it isn't. That tree out there isn't science.
>
> Parent: Yes it is because… (provides an explanation)
>
> Child: Well, this chair isn't science.
>
> Parent: Yes it is because…(gives an explanation touching on forces and materials)
>
> Child: The wall isn't science.
>
> And so on!

This was an argument that the child could never win, because science *is* everywhere and everything. And yet the enormous potential for enhancing teaching and learning in science through outdoor activities and experiences is largely untapped (ASE, 2007), and outdoor education has been in decline (House of Commons, 2005).

Progress is being made. As the ASE (2007) pointed out in their contribution to the Primary Review:

> The advent of the Outdoor Manifesto, the continuing activities of the Real World Learning campaign and the drive to address issues of sustainable development in science education all point to the need to encourage greater use of the outdoors in science teaching and learning.

The 'Learning Outside the Classroom Manifesto' (DfES, 2006) (also referred to as the 'Outdoor Manifesto') states that every young person should experience the world beyond the classroom as an essential part of learning and personal development. The justification for learning to take place beyond the classroom is in place and is strong. Our task is to turn the recommendations into practice. There is a growing body of good quality advice and guidance to support us in this. For example, Real World Learning, a partnership between organizations providing out-of-school education such as the RSBPB, The Field Studies Council, The Wetlands Trust, The National Trust and PGL (see the website for a full list of partners) have produced a booklet (available online) that outlines a wide range of out-of-classroom opportunities, many specifying links to the science curriculum. It provides invaluable guidance for teachers on how to plan and organize outdoor learning. The ASE is also a useful source of information and ideas.

So children can – and do – learn science very effectively in and from 'beyond school' contexts such as museums and galleries, farms, reserves, historical houses and national parks. The learning of science can also be enhanced by simply locating activity beyond the classroom. Large-scale science activities can necessitate a move outside and convey the benefits of outdoor learning. The children will be investigating, exploring and problem-solving on a much larger scale than usual; such activities often have a profound and lasting impact. Possibilities for large-scale science include: giant bubbles (from hoops inside a paddling pool of bubble mixture); enormous soda fountains (by dropping mints into bottles of cola); rockets from washing-up liquid bottles; boxes with 'cargo' to be transported... a plethora of ideas are available from published resources and the internet.

> Education is not something to keep in a box, even when the box is classroom-shaped.
> (Real World Learning Partnership, 2006)

Scientists are real people!

You will be familiar with the stereotypical image of a scientist: a middle-aged man, wearing a white coat, with wild hair (or alternatively, with a bald dome of a head), holding a test tube or a smoking flask. The image is ubiquitous, and study after study confirms its continuance (for example, Bradley, 2001; Jane et al, 2007). This is not to say that children believe that scientists actually *do* look like this: if interviewed after drawing a scientist, they will tend to qualify what they have done by saying that that they had to draw it that way so the researchers would recognize it (Jane et al, 2007)! However, what I believe should be of concern to teachers is the fact that this stereotype may be present very early, *before* children begin compulsory education.

Fgure9.1 shows a 6-year-old child's drawing of 'a scientist', with their description below. Figure 9.2 was drawn by a 3-year-old child and here, the discussion with the child after drawing was telling: the double lines for legs indicate trousers, and the person in the drawing is holding two quite strange objects. Already this child seems to be associating science with males and eccentric behaviours.

Being aware of the scale of the issue will go some way to helping you to address it effectively, but it is unlikely to be sufficient to model 'being a scientist' yourself. Make links with scientists and invite them into school to take part in science lessons (that is, working alongside the children, not only 'giving a talk'); ensure that the scientists represent different genders and cultures and different areas of science; arrange visits to science-focused places of work; tell the stories of real people working in science (ancient and modern – and not solely Marie Curie); and encourage the children to role-play scientists and their (the scientists') daily lives. Your task is to enable the children to understand that science is about *their* lives too, and that it is carried out by people just like them.

Figure 1, by M aged 6
'He's a scientist and he's holding a hamster and a jar.'

Figure 2, by J aged 3
'A scientist with spiky hair and he's got salt and a rock with trousers on.'

Figures 9.1 and 9.2 Drawings of a scientist

Celebrating and promoting science

Opportunities abound for promoting and developing science, not only within the school but throughout the school's community and beyond.

The British Association for the Advancement of Science (the BA) offer the CREST Star Investigators' programme. Children work through a series of fun, easily-resourced and enquiry-focused activities in science clubs within their school (see www.the-BA.net). The power of such extra-curricular sessions to generate enthusiasm for and interest in a subject in both children and parents should not be underestimated. Children only spend 14 per cent of their time in schools in any year (Balls, 2007), so any time you invest in involving parents in children's learning is well spent. Science activities lend themselves very well to 'drop-in' sessions during parents' evenings and after-school-hours events, showcasing activities which can be carried out at home and, more importantly, generating discussion of science concepts within families. The BA also coordinate National Science and Engineering Week, with full and varied programmes of events in all regions of the country (details from website, as above).

Science contributes to a culture of *enterprise* very effectively. This is increasingly becoming a focus in schools throughout the UK. 'Enterprise in Education' is a cross-curricular element of the 5 to 14 curriculum in Scotland, and 'Determined to Succeed' is a strategy for delivering this. It is not about teaching enterprise skills in specific classes or expecting all children to become entrepreneurs: its focus is on enabling children to gain self-confidence and the ability to think creatively, embedding enterprise education in the curriculum and school life (www.scotland.gov.uk/topic/education/schools/curriculum/ 5to14). These aims accord well with the aims of science education. Enterprise in education benefits from the creation of strong links with businesses and external organizations. These links can be facilitated by involvement in awards schemes for primary science, such as the Rolls Royce prize or the Astra Zeneca Primary Science Teacher Awards.

A North West primary school created a community library of lending resources for primary science in the form of 'science sacks', with activities following a storyline, illustrating science concepts and linking to real world applications. This was a winner in the Rolls Royce Science Prize scheme (see www.science.rolls-royce.com).

Conclusion

This chapter has discussed going (far) beyond the statutory curriculum for science. The discussion has not focused solely on 'cross-curricular' links: there is much to be gained from meaningful links being made between areas of learning, such as science and literacy, science and mathematics, and science and design and technology. And there is plenty of guidance and support available. For example, the ASE website has ready-prepared 'maps' linking science, mathematics and literacy in England's Primary Framework. (A degree of caution must be exercised when looking for resources, as many 'exciting' lessons often turn out to be worksheet-based, and the internet is not infallible.)

As education in the twenty-first century dares to move out of subject boxes and into different ways of conceptualizing the experience and content of learning – for children and their teachers – we must be thinking in terms of interconnections and extended opportunities, preparing our children to take their places in a rapidly changing, constantly challenging and exciting global society.

References

Association for Science Education (ASE) (2007), *The Primary Review: Submission of Evidence from the Association for Science Education*. Executive Summary. Hatfield: ASE.

Balls, E. (2007), 'Balls' Juggling Act.' *Guardian*, 6 September.

Bradley, D. (2001), 'Uncool Boffins: All children's perceptions of scientists.' Biomednet.com. 11 May 2001.

Department for Children, Schools and Families (2007), *Early Years Foundation Stage*. London: DCSF.

Department for Education and Skills (2006), 'Learning Outside the Classroom Manifesto.' London: DfES.

Department for International Development (DFID) (2006), *Developing the Global Dimension in the School Curriculum*. London: DfES/DFID.

Feasey, R. (1999), *Science and Literacy Links*. Hatfield: ASE.

House of Commons Education and Skills Committee (2005), *Education Outside the Classroom; Second Report of Session 2004–2005*. London: HMSO.

Jane, B., Fleer, M. and Gipps, J. (2007), 'Changing children's views of science and scientists through school-based teaching.' *Asia-Pacific Forum on Science Learning and Teaching* 8 (1).

Mahy, M. (1987), *The Boy with Two Shadows*. London: Collins.

National Advisory Committee on Creative and Cultural Education (NACCCE) (1999), *All Our Futures: Creativity, Culture and Education*. London: DCSF.

NOP World Research (2004), www.wrap.org.uk (Accessed February 2007.)

Real World Learning Partnership (2006), *Out-of-classroom Learning: Practical Information and Guidance for Schools and Teachers*. RWL: www.field-studio.council.org

Scottish Consultative Council on the Curriculum (1996), *Teaching for Effective Learning*. Dundee: SCCC.

Teachernet. *Sustainable Schools*. www.teachernet.gov.uk/sustainableschools (Accessed February 2007.)

Websites

The Association for Science Education (ASE) www.ase.org.uk

The BA (British Association for the Advancement of Science) www.the-BA.net

Concept cartoons www.conceptcarttons.com (supported by GlaxoSmithKline)

Eco-Schools www.eco-schools.org.uk

Real World Learning Partnership www.field-studies-council.org

Teaching Information and Communication Technology: The Principles

Nick Easingwood

To err is human – and to blame it on a computer is even more so.
(Orben, 2000)

Introduction

Unlike the other core subject areas of English, mathematics and science, information and communication technology (ICT) is a relatively recent addition to the primary curriculum. Largely non-existent in most primary schools before 1983, the introduction of the computer to English schools, along with the rapid and corresponding technological advances in society since the mid-1980s, has had a significant effect on primary practice. In most schools ICT has had a profound impact on learning and teaching. The purpose of the next three chapters is to explore the principles, the practice and the further potential of ICT to transform the primary curriculum, and the processes of learning and teaching within them.

The ability of even the youngest children to use a wide range of modern technologies should call into question the very place and purpose of the primary school as we know it today. It is the power of these technologies – such as the ability to connect to the internet from anywhere, the creative use of interactive whiteboards (IWBs), or moving a programmable toy around the room – that is having a wide-reaching and profound effect on the way that learning and teaching occurs and, in turn, how it is organized and delivered.

The place of ICT in the primary curriculum

At first glance the complexity of today's highly technological society could make a precise definition of the role of ICT within primary education difficult. Along with the development of portable mobile technologies (such as telephones, laptops and handheld devices), as well as the parallel widespread use of entertainment technologies (such as digital satellite television on demand, video games, DVDs and CDs, MP3 players, digital still and video cameras), the introduction of ICT in general, and the computer in particular, has had a profound impact upon all of our lives. For the primary school child growing up at the start of the twenty-first century, using this technology provides everyday opportunities and possibilities that were in the realms of science fiction only a generation before. Placed into the wider context of the use of technology in society, it might seem relatively straightforward to define the role that ICT should have in our primary schools, in that it should be used to prepare individuals to play a full and active role in society through creating ICT literate citizens. While this is undoubtedly true, this is a somewhat simplistic view of the reasons for using ICT, and barely begins to do justice to the power that it can bring to learning and teaching. The notion that society needs skilled technology operators and that schools should prepare children for future employment where using a computer will be an essential part of their future occupations may essentially be true, but ICT can offer primary schools, their teachers, and in particular their children, so much more. This includes:

- providing opportunities for 'value-added' experiences
- providing a dynamic, creative and interactive teaching and learning environment
- providing a focus for collaborative and investigative learning
- acting as a tool for investigative learning
- acting as a labour-saving device
- allowing access to higher levels of learning
- acting as a means of motivating children.

These roles are by no means mutually exclusive. A creative and imaginatively constructed lesson that is using ICT may well contain some or even all of these elements to a greater or lesser degree, and this is illustrated by the examples detailed below. It could be argued that these are the elements that help to compose *all* good lessons, not just those involving

ICT. What cannot be denied, however, is the fact that the power of technology, which was once confined to the world of commerce and industry, is now available to primary education. The true challenge is in determining how this power can be harnessed and used productively in the primary setting.

The historical development of ICT in the primary curriculum

The strong influence of ICT upon teaching and learning is largely due to the fact that it is both a separate, discrete subject and a cross-curricular tool. This dual role has been explicitly reinforced in England since the introduction of ICT into the first National Curriculum in 1989 (DES, 1989). Its presence within the current curriculum is even more significant.

Although there have been other 'new' subjects introduced since the first National Curriculum, in truth these have been little more than traditional subjects being re-packaged under a new name. For example, woodwork and metalwork became the 'resistant materials' strand of design technology; home economics (and before that, domestic science) became food technology; and technical drawing became graphics.

Before the 1980s, computers were rarely seen outside of university science or mathematics departments, so their arrival in the primary classroom was a genuinely new experience. Initially information technology (IT), as it was then known, was a sub-section of the design and technology document: but the second version of the National Curriculum in 1995 detailed it as a completely separate subject for the first time. ICT's status was further reinforced in 1999 by the third incarnation of the National Curriculum, which came into use in England in 2000. This added 'Communication' to ICT (DfEE, 1999). Pedagogically important, it was introduced to describe the interactive and communicative nature of the subject, and to reinforce the fact that children should be active rather than passive users of technology.

The continual development of ICT as part of the National Curriculum was a highly significant move, as before the mid-1990s it had a troubled evolution. ICT in English primary education had a very slow start, with the period 1983 to 1997 demonstrating relatively little development in terms of the pedagogy of the subject, staff training, and provision of hardware and software. Despite the fact that the respective National Curriculum documents have demanded pupil entitlement to ICT, the development of the use of the computer in schools has been somewhat patchy and piecemeal. This has been mainly due to both variations in funding at both national and local levels (which impacted upon training opportunities and equipment provision), and perceived priorities within individual schools.

Initially each school, regardless of size, was given half-funding for one computer, usually a BBC-B microcomputer. Curiously, and perhaps reflecting the priorities of the Conservative government at the time, the money came from the Department for Trade and Industry rather than the Department for Education and Science. Developed by Acorn Computers in Cambridge in 1981, the BBC-B was extremely primitive by modern standards; but when they started to appear in schools in 1983 they were state of the art and represented a quantum leap forward in technology. Many primary schools saw the potential that they offered immediately, but were unable to exploit it due to the fact that there was often only one computer between several classes, and very few members of staff knew how to use it (or wanted to do so). There were also frequent technical problems, usually concerning the tape recorder that was used to load the programs (which were stored on cassette tapes) onto the computer. This could take several minutes and seldom worked first time. Although this seems laughable by today's standards, at the time it was the only way to load a program onto a computer.

As most primary school classes only saw the computer once a week, the pedagogy of ICT tended to be based around simple drill and practice games, which required only a simple yes or no or numerical answer (interestingly many of these games still exist and are known as Interactive Teaching Programs, available as downloads from the DfES website specifically for use with IWBs). The lack of equipment and training for staff, the perceived need to expose as many children to the computer in as short a time as possible, as well as the belief that the very presence of the computer in the classroom was sufficient, ensured that a clear pedagogy for ICT took many years to develop. When appropriate pedagogy did start to emerge in the mid-1980s, it was based around teachers being taught how to write programs for the computer. The theory for this was that teachers would be able to author content that was specific to the needs of their pupils. This philosophy was clearly never going to be successful. The majority of teachers simply did not have the time, inclination or technical ability to do this. Such commercial programs that did exist were poor (as they were usually written by professional programmers rather than teachers or educators), slow to load and pedagogically unsound.

However, a growing number of teachers discovered an application that genuinely provided interactive teaching and learning opportunities. LOGO, developed by Seymour Papert at Massachusetts Institute of Technology (MIT), enables the user to control a screen or floor turtle through using a series of commands. This was the first instance of open-ended software being available to children, where the user was controlling the computer rather than the other way round. This particular application is at its most effective when the children can work collaboratively and talk about their work, drawing patterns, shapes or pictures. The finished work is not great art – but that is not the point: what is important is the act of discussing where lines should be drawn, what angle they should be and how long they should be.

As the pedagogy for ICT developed, so did the technology. By the early 1990s the first windows-based computers were appearing in schools, with vastly enhanced graphics capabilities, small and robust plastic floppy disks and CD-ROMs. The CD-ROMs in particular enabled much larger programs to be installed, complete with hyperlinked, searchable and professional-looking text, graphics and even short video clips with sound. Although visually impressive, some of these were pedagogically and educationally lacking, largely relying on children watching the content rather than directly interacting with it. In many respects, the introduction of more modern computers actually set back the place and purpose of educational ICT, in that the truly interactive activities (such as LOGO) were left behind in favour of the more visually impressive CD-ROMs.

Throughout the 1990s the BBC computers were replaced by computers made by Acorn, Apple or PCs running Microsoft windows. By this time there was usually at least one computer in every primary classroom. Although pupils had regular access to ICT, it was not always regular enough, and wide-scale training for teachers was often lacking. There were also reliability issues with some computers, which led to many teachers becoming increasingly disillusioned with the technology, as well as frustrated by the lack of appropriate software.

Principles of good practice

In the 1980s and early 1990s it was often assumed that the very presence of ICT in the classroom would lead to learning situations developing and happening naturally. There were even suggestions that computers would somehow replace teachers. While this may well now be technologically possible in some instances, it certainly represents a highly undesirable way of teaching. In order for this to happen, the model of learning and teaching would have to be based closely upon a scenario where the computer was in control of the child rather than the other way round. In order for ICT to be used most effectively, the children need to be using ICT in an interactive and dynamic way. Automation without a teacher cannot and will not do this. A computer cannot ask specific, yet open-ended questions that are focused on the individual learners and their learning; nor can it respond to children's questions safely and securely, providing detailed and accurate answers that move the children's learning forward.

However, 1997 proved to be the watershed year. The publication of two seminal documents, the Stevenson Report (1997) and *Connecting the Learning Society* (DfEE, 1997) as well as the election of a Labour government, represented a turning point for ICT in English primary schools. These documents were used to inform the new government's education policy, and consequently a large amount of state funding ensured that every primary school in the country could afford to equip itself with a sufficient amount of hardware, and also provided training for every member of staff. This included giving every child and teacher an email address, financing internet access and developing the notion of a National Grid for Learning, whereby all educational institutions such as libraries, schools and universities would be linked together via the internet. The training was given to every member of the teaching profession, and was based on pedagogy as opposed to ICT key skills.

The clear pedagogical framework that underpinned the training programmes came from two sources: the New Opportunities Fund (NOF), and Government Circular 4/98, *High Status, High Standards* (DfEE, 1998), which was the first curriculum for initial teacher training. Both used the same criteria to ensure that all practitioners would be trained to the same standard, thus ensuring continuity and progression. Although 4/98 has been superseded twice, the ICT requirements of 4/98 and the NOF-funded training provided the clear pedagogical framework that underpins ICT teaching in English primary schools today. The key pedagogical reasons for using ICT are:

- interactivity
- provisionality
- capacity and range
- speed and automatic function.

These four factors underpin how ICT should be taught in school, and provide a strong pedagogical basis for teaching and learning.

Interactivity

Interactivity should take three distinct forms within lessons where ICT is used. First, lessons should involve the child's interaction with the computer, other children and the teacher. This however should not be mutually exclusive, in that the teacher must also make a point of interacting with the pupils, although not necessarily with the computer – that is the role of the pupil. The child should act as a conduit between computer and teacher, with the teacher's role being to engage and encourage children through the use of open-ended questions such as:

- That looks interesting, tell me about it.
- I like what you have produced there, how did you do it?
- Why did you do it like that?
- If you were to do that again, would you do it any differently?
- Why?

It is through effective questioning that learning is reinforced and enhanced.

Second, it is crucial that the kind of activities that are set lend themselves to interactivity. There is little point in using 'drill and practise programs' that simply require the child to respond with a closed answer that will be right or wrong, with a happy face or jolly tune indicating that the answer was correct. Although these programs may have their uses with children needing continual practice and reinforcement of key concepts, it is highly unlikely that they will offer anything that cannot be delivered more effectively by more traditional means.

Third, the computer is at its most effective as a learning resource when it is being used by the children as a tool to further their learning, or where it is being used as an open-ended creative device. Examples of the former might include using a word processing package to write stories, newspapers or poems; databases to handle and manipulate data; and digital cameras and scanners to record their work. Examples of the latter include LOGO, control technology and web page design. In both cases the child is in control of the technology, and although there can never be software that is entirely content-free, the child is effectively programming the computer to achieve his or her required aims.

Provisionality

This is where any work produced by ICT is never completely permanent. It can be edited, redrafted and developed at any point, and can be worked on by many different children. When the internet and email are taken into account, this can take place within a class, within other classes in the same school, the school down the road or indeed a school anywhere in the world. The advantage of this is that work can be developed by as many or as few children as is necessary.

Capacity and range

The capacity of ICT refers to the amount of information and data that the computer can deal with; the range represents the many different uses that ICT can be put to. In the primary school, this will involve harnessing the ability of ICT to take many different forms, which can operate either separately or simultaneously. For example, a computer can run the following software applications:

- word processing
- presentations
- databases
- desktop publishing
- spreadsheets

- graphics and animation packages
- LOGO
- video editing packages.

It includes surfing the internet, using email and manipulating images captured by digital scanner, camera or downloaded from the internet. It can also be used for more specialist applications, such as data-logging and control technology.

The key point to remember is that these different applications can be used either as stand-alone activities or integrated with other pieces of software. Additionally, an added advantage is that the key skills necessary to use one piece of software are often transferable to others, enabling the user to become proficient in a range of software more quickly.

Speed and automatic function

In many ways these two elements are directly related to capacity and range. Speed and automation truly represent the power of ICT, in that a computer and associated peripherals can perform all of its functions extremely quickly – often instantly – and automatically. Harnessing these aspects means that pupils can access higher levels of learning and understanding, as the computer can remove the drudgery of many manual and menial tasks.

The place of ICT as a tool for collaborative and investigative learning

Another key role for ICT is that it can act as a suitable vehicle for a wide range of collaborative and investigative learning situations. In the same way that the point above discusses the critical importance of ICT as a dynamic, interactive activity, so should it promote both collaboration and investigation. These two are deliberately linked here; good primary practice often dictates that one can not exist without the other.

Collaborative learning

Collaborative learning should always be an educational rather than an organizational device; that is, children should be working together on a shared activity as opposed to sitting together as a group but working individually on the same activity. Whether collaboration is genuinely taking place or not can be crudely tested by removing one of the individuals from the task. If the dynamics and the nature of the task are significantly altered, then this task can probably be said to have been collaborative. If not, then it probably was not collaborative in the first place.

Although children can pursue investigative tasks on an individual basis, they are much more effective when there are at least two pupils involved. This allows for interaction between child and computer, child and teacher, teacher and computer, but also between child and child. This is fundamentally important in allowing pupils to formulate their own ideas, and follow an investigation through to its logical conclusion. The computer then takes a lower profile in the relationship, providing the *means* of collaboration and investigation rather than becoming the focus of the lesson. This is a particular danger if the lesson is being taught in an ICT suite, where 20 or so computers can overemphasize the importance of the computer. The role of the teacher then becomes important in that they need to facilitate investigation, rather than dominate it. It is particularly helpful if laptops or any other portable devices are being used, especially outside of the classroom. Consider the example of word processing. There are plenty of opportunities here to develop collaborative learning, and when exploiting other aspects of technology, the authors do not even have to be in the same country, let alone the same room.

ICT as a tool for investigative learning

Collaborative learning also reduces significantly the risk of children becoming isolated in front of a computer, where they might become passive recipients of material on the screen, rather than genuinely interacting with it and using it as a tool to support their own investigations. It is not desirable in any way for primary-aged children to be sitting in front of a screen, perhaps wearing headphones, and simply following a series of prescriptive, on-screen instructions; or, even worse, watching a video or DVD that in no way allows any creative interaction or participation in decision making. What is important is that children are sharing ideas and advice, composing work on the screen, entering data and processing it into information, capturing images with a digital camera and editing these on screen, or using Boolean logic and logical operators to search for information on the internet.

ICT acting as a labour-saving device

For children

One of the key elements of the child being in control of the computer is the fact that they are by definition using it as a labour-saving device. We have already seen that one of the key advantages of using a computer is that it can handle a large amount of data quickly and easily, rapidly processing it in a number of different ways into information that can then be used for further analysis or insertion into any other document (such as a report, presentation or web page). Harnessing this power is important and means that the time saved by using a computer can be more effectively used by concentrating on other aspects of learning. For example, children might collect their own data from a traffic survey, which they then input into a data-handling application. The data can then be processed with the facility to produce graphs and charts from the resulting information. Rather than spending much time laboriously drawing graphs and colouring in the bars, the time can be more efficiently spent analysing the results.

Although it is important for children to draw graphs by hand – this is the only way that they will truly understand what graphs are, how they are constructed and what their properties are – this does not need to be done every time that there is a need for a graph to be produced. Drawing a new type of graph once ensures comprehension, but subsequent graphing activities can be completed on a computer.

For teachers

Teachers can benefit from the use of ICT just as much as the children that they teach. This takes two forms: in the preparation of materials for learning and teaching, and for administrative tasks, including the production of lesson plans and pupils' records, and writing reports.

One of the teachers' most time-consuming tasks has traditionally been planning lessons and materials for learning and teaching: but computers, and particularly the internet, have made this considerably easier. A wide range of professional-looking materials can be created very quickly – regardless of whether ICT is being used in the lesson or not. This includes worksheets, work cards, pictures, tables and charts, with the teachers authoring the resources themselves or getting them from other sources such as other colleagues in the school, or via the internet through appropriate websites or discussion forums (permissions and copyright permitting). These can then be saved in a folder, along with the accompanying lesson plans and other relevant material, such as multimedia PowerPoint presentations. Over a period of time the teacher will have produced and collected a vast range of appropriate material that will not need to be created from scratch each time a particular topic or subject needs to be taught. Instead, the teacher will be focused on amending, updating and editing this existing material to suit the particular classes and individuals who are being taught. This will ensure that the resulting resources and materials are more specifically geared to the individual needs of the pupil concerned. Clearly, the initial production of the materials will take time – but then it would anyway regardless of whether ICT was being used or not. It is a sound investment of time that will pay dividends as time passes. One additional advantage is that this material can immediately be posted onto the schools website or into a virtual learning environment (VLE) for access both inside and outside of school. In the case of a multimedia PowerPoint presentation, it can be viewed online or, in the case of worksheets, completed and submitted to the teacher electronically for marking and assessment. This form of e-learning is an extremely powerful and efficient way of working.

Records of assessments can also be accurately and efficiently kept and maintained on a computer. Teachers can type assessments into a table on word processing or spreadsheet software. These can be informed directly from the online National Curriculum and National Curriculum in Action websites. Selected features of the records can then be copied and pasted into documents, and these can form the basis of reports to parents on their child's attainment.

ICT as a means of motivating children

One very important, but easily underestimated, role of ICT is that of motivation. Most children enjoy using a wide range of modern technologies, such as mobile phones, MP3 players and digital cameras. These are an every day part of life for young people. This interest and enthusiasm can also be captured for use in the school. The results of the Impact2 project found that children could remain on task for up to 50 per cent longer when using ICT and, significantly, could also raise their levels of achievement across the curriculum. This should come as little surprise; if children are encouraged to use ICT in the way described above, they will be developing all of the correct approaches to learning that forms the basis of effective primary practice.

Conclusion

This chapter has identified the key principles concerning the place and purpose of ICT in the primary school curriculum. All aspects of an effective pedagogy are critically important if ICT is to be taught well, but especially the principle of interactivity. ICT must provide a dynamic, interactive learning and teaching environment at all times, otherwise it will become a one-way, didactic exercise where the computer is reduced to the level of a teaching machine, with the children reduced to passive observers of whatever is displayed on the screen. The next chapter will describe how these important elements of theory can be put into every day practice.

References

Department for Education and Employment (1997), *Connecting the Learning Society*. National Grid for Learning, Government Consultation Paper. London: DfEE.

Department for Education and Employment (1998), *High Status, High Standards*. Circular Number 4/98. London: DfEE.

Department for Education and Employment (1999), *The National Curriculum: Handbook for Primary Teachers in England*. London: DfEE/QCA.

Department Education and Science (1989), *National Curriculum for England and Wales*. London: HMSO.

Orben, R. (2000), *Speaker's Handbook of Humour.* London: Merriam Webster.

The Stevenson Commission Report (1997), 'Information and Communications Technology in UK Schools: An Independent Inquiry.' London: The Cabinet Office.

11 Teaching Information and Communication Technology: The Practice

Nick Easingwood

They take to [ICT] like ducks to water. They seem quite fearless in the way they will explore, investigate and discuss what happens.

(Year 1 teacher)

Introduction

In Chapter 10 we discussed the principles of teaching and learning ICT in the primary school curriculum. We identified the dual roles that ICT has within the curriculum and the reasons for its presence there. We also examined the impact of ICT on the context for learning and teaching, and recognized how ICT can enhance the power of collaborative learning and investigative learning. In this chapter we will attempt to take these key principles and identify the most important aspect of all, which is how they can be delivered in practice.

As with all other areas of the curriculum, the most effective learning cannot possibly take place without good teaching that is based upon secure pedagogical principles. In the case of ICT, Government Circular 4/98, *High Status, High Standards* (DfES, 1998) provided a strong pedagogical foundation through identifying the means to capture and use the power that it offers in terms of interactivity, provisionality, and harnessing the computers' advantages of speed and automatic function, as well as capacity and range. When the ability to motivate pupils is added to this, it is clear to see that there are many reasons why ICT should be used. These immense advantages do, however, place a great deal of responsibility upon the teacher to use ICT 'properly'. When coupled with the need to also include an effective pedagogy from any other subject that may be involved, it can be seen that teaching using ICT is potentially a very complex business indeed. It could be argued that difficulties might arise when the pedagogy of ICT directly contradicts the pedagogy of the subject that it is supporting. This however should not be the case, as effective ICT teaching is no different from teaching any other subject: there should be interactivity and interest in all lessons.

Preparing to teach ICT

Primary teachers, as generalists who are usually also trained to teach the full range of primary age children, continuously seek to ensure that their practice is effective. However, we are also aware that achieving excellence in all areas of the curriculum is challenging, especially with the constant changes to the curriculum that have always been a continuous part of the educational process.

While the recent inclusion of ICT into the curriculum has been positive, emphasis has sometimes been placed on 'mastering the machinery' rather than on consideration of the specific pedagogical knowledge necessary for teaching ICT well. As a practitioner you will be aware that this, and several other aspects of practice, need consideration before we consider embarking on the planning, teaching and assessing cycle for this subject.

Pedagogical Awareness

Understanding and knowledge of an appropriate pedagogy is the first and most important point to consider when ICT is to be taught. Initially, a teacher needs to be absolutely clear as to the roles ICT will play within their practice.

ICT has two quite distinct pedagogical roles within the curriculum. It can be taught as:

- a curriculum subject in its own right, and taught as a discrete ICT lesson; or
- a cross-curricular tool to support learning and teaching in another curriculum area.

These two different roles mean two different approaches will need to be used when planning, teaching and assessing for learning and teaching. A discrete ICT lesson will have an emphasis on the development of ICT key skills, and have specific objectives to reflect this. Alternatively, when ICT is supporting another subject (for example, maths or science), planning will have the objectives that are specific to that particular subject: there may well be secondary objectives that are ICT based, but primarily the focus will be on the specific subject that is being taught. This curriculum awareness is a key factor, as otherwise there may be an inappropriate emphasis on ICT at the expense of the subject being taught.

At this stage you are probably thinking that we are stating the obvious: but let us consider a relatively straightforward example of classroom practice, involving the use of a word processing package.

Children can compose stories, poems or newspaper articles on the screen, either individually or in pairs, which they can then edit easily, perhaps changing the colour and size of the text, or changing the font to make the work more visually striking; they can insert images, either in the form of clipart downloaded from the internet or images that they themselves have taken with a digital camera or via a scanner. This in itself would be virtually impossible without the use of both the appropriate hardware and the associated software; the text could not be changed, and any pictures would have to be cut out of magazines or printed in order to be glued onto the page. The ability to use a computer to produce a neat and professional looking piece of work that shows no rubbings out or deletions, or indeed any trace of the many steps that it might have gone through, is a powerful thing indeed.

So, how are you going to teach the children in your class the skills they need to use this software effectively?

- If you teach the skills in an English lesson you would have both a context and purpose for using the ICT software, but in an English lesson the main objective of this lesson is, obviously, to teach English.
- If you teach them in a discrete ICT lesson, what will provide the context and purpose for using a word processing package?

Once you have a clear understanding of the status of ICT within your lessons, planning will become less problematic. From the discussion above you will have identified that the general rules will be:

- To *teach* new skills in a discrete lesson using the relevant content from another subject area. Children should be familiar with this subject matter so that it does not detract from the ICT skill being taught.
- To *practise* the new skill in the subject area in which it is most appropriate, and recognize that the role of ICT is to support that subject.

It is evident that much of your organizational planning for ICT will need to be at the long- and medium-term levels, so that you can coordinate subjects that will allow you both to teach ICT and to provide opportunities for children to practise their skills.

The importance of subject knowledge

Teaching a discrete ICT lesson

When teaching ICT as a discrete subject, it is essential that as well as pedagogical knowledge all teachers have appropriate levels of ICT subject knowledge. This includes:

- being able to manage the hardware you will be using. This could include computers, interactive whiteboards (IWBs), digital/ordinary cameras, digital microscopes and programmable toys
- being familiar with the contents of the software you are using
- being able to use the software competently
- being aware of any protocols and safety issues relevant to the use of ICT: for example inappropriate internet websites, and cyber bullying (see Chapter 12 for more information).

As a result of ICT's dependency on the content of other subjects to provide purpose for its use, the level of a teacher's knowledge of other subjects will also influence the effectiveness of teaching in a discrete ICT lesson.

An excellent example of the need for a detailed and wide-ranging subject knowledge occurs when teaching children to use a LOGO package. This particular ICT lesson requires in-depth knowledge of several key areas of ICT: knowing how to use the LOGO software, which by today's standards can often feel clumsy and 'clunky' to use; knowing how to use LOGO hardware such as a floor turtle; and also the pedagogy of how LOGO should be taught. However, it is critically important to have a good mathematical knowledge, particularly in the areas of geometry, distance, angles, direction and bearings, shape and space, and number bonds. With older primary age children, quite complex geometrical shapes can be produced using LOGO, so it is necessary for the teacher to be able to ask the right questions and set appropriate tasks in order to reinforce and extend children's learning. The teacher needs to have clear expectations of what he or she wants the children to produce during the lesson; and for this to happen, excellent knowledge of all aspects of using the hardware, software and potential outcomes is essential – as is a detailed knowledge of the children. What they have achieved, and what they are capable of achieving is also crucial to the process.

Teaching ICT within another subject

When using ICT to support another subject, there are other components that need to be considered. These are:

- the subject knowledge for ICT
- the pedagogy for ICT

- the subject knowledge for the curriculum area that is being taught
- the pedagogy for the subject that is being supported by the use of ICT.

It might be easy to underestimate the importance of subject knowledge, particularly in the primary phase: but this is one of the most important aspects of primary practitioners' professional expertise. The ability to answer children's questions safely and securely, provide them with specialist subject knowledge and understanding, extend the more able children and support the less able is crucial to effective teaching, and can only be done with detailed subject knowledge and pedagogical understanding. The added difficulty for the primary teacher is, as already stated, the necessity to have expertise in every subject of the curriculum.

The nature of primary teaching is such that quite apart from intended learning outcomes (that is, learning that was intended when the lesson was planned), there may well be unintended learning outcomes, or learning from curriculum areas that might not have been foreseen at the outset. This is always likely in any lesson where there is a cross-curricular element, and particularly when ICT is being used as a research tool. The spontaneous nature of both ICT and the primary curriculum are clear strengths, but they also provide teachers with potential problems concerning the need to have wide-ranging subject knowledge.

Planning for ICT

As in all lessons, effective learning and teaching can only occur where there has been careful and appropriate planning and preparation. ICT is no exception. As a practitioner you will be aware that all three levels of planning (long-term, medium-term and short-term) are essential.

Long-term and medium-term planning

In England the National Curriculum (DfEE,1999) details *what* should be taught, but does not specify *when* different aspects of ICT should be taught (beyond the allocation to a Key Stage). It is at the long- and medium-term levels of planning that whole school decisions need to be made, in order to ensure coverage and progression of the whole ICT curriculum. In some schools the planning of the scheme of work will be done by the ICT subject leader; and in others (usually small schools), it is done through the collaboration of all staff members. An increasing number of schools now use the non-statutory schemes of work developed by the Qualifications and Curriculum Authority (QCA) to inform both their long- and medium-term planning. The organization of the units contained in these schemes of work allows all practitioners to clearly see the progression and coverage of the subject throughout the school.

As already stated, because of the relationship of ICT to other subjects in the curriculum, long- and medium-term plans are important. It is at these levels that the links that need to be made to other subjects can be planned so that they are relevant and purposeful. The units contained in the schemes of work also provide plenty of excellent ideas, especially for the teacher who perhaps has less confidence in his or her subject knowledge.

Short-term planning for ICT

In some schools short-term planning is a weekly plan, and in others it may be a brief single lesson plan. Whichever model the school uses, when planning at this level the teacher needs to ensure that all of the aspects discussed in this chapter so far are fully and completely considered, as these underpin what makes a good ICT lesson. Detailed subject knowledge and a full appreciation of the pedagogy of ICT are essential for this. As a consequence, the lesson plan needs to include the following key components:

- the main aims and the key themes of the lesson
- the identification of cross-curricular links
- the learning objectives
- the learning outcomes
- differentiation strategies, including the identification of pupils with special needs
- resources for the lesson
- contingency plans
- assessment strategies.

Attention should also be paid to the three teaching and learning elements of the lesson, that is, the introduction, the work phase and the plenary. As an integral part of the lesson, consideration should be given to both the teacher's activity and the children's activity. What will each be doing? What will their respective roles be?

The main aims and the key themes of the lesson

This is where the teacher identifies the purpose of the lesson: either a discrete ICT lesson, or a subject-specific lesson where ICT is being used. This will usually be informed by the school's long- and medium-term planning, which in England will in turn have been informed by a national document such as the National Curriculum for England, the QCA schemes of work or the Primary Strategy.

The identification of cross-curricular links

This is the section where any cross-curricular links can be explicitly identified. Even in a discrete ICT lesson, it is highly likely that there will be at least some aspects of the lesson that will directly connect to another aspect of the curriculum. This will usually be literacy or mathematics, but not necessarily. Other examples might include science or geography (data-logging), modern languages (the internet and email), and history (digital video editing). Consideration also needs to be given to any aspect of the National Curriculum for these subjects that might be met through an attainment target.

Learning objectives

Selecting appropriate learning objectives for ICT needs greater consideration than most other subjects. Although cross-curricular teaching has led to greater inter-subjective practice between subjects, ICT, as we have already discussed, has a more dominant relationship with other subjects. In all discrete ICT lessons, precise and specific learning objectives based mainly on the ICT curriculum will be needed. The use of ICT learning objectives in other lessons using ICT will be at the practitioner's discretion, and depends on the main aims of the lesson.

There should be a maximum of three objectives. While these could be taken from the scheme of work it is advised that they are made more specific and relevant to the needs of your own class and to the children's prior knowledge.

The learning outcomes

These are the intended learning outcomes for the lesson, and are usually defined in one of three ways:

- Most children will.....
- Some children will not have made so much progress and will...
- Some children will have progressed further and will...

These will indicate what the pupils will have achieved by the end of the lesson, and will also inform your assessment.

Inclusive practices

In this section you consider how you will address the needs of children who need extra support (this will be discussed in more detail in the next part of this chapter).

Resources for the lesson

This will of course depend on the location and type of lesson, but generally speaking will invariably involve computers! The teacher, however, needs to give careful consideration here to the preparation of the resources, rather than to getting them together in the first place (since lessons will often mean using the ICT suite where they will be permanently located). However, you need to check that:

- the printers are loaded with sufficient paper and ink
- the computers are working
- the network is working
- the interactive whiteboard is working
- a risk assessment has been undertaken – no trailing cables, no bare wires, the light is not shining on monitors, chairs are correctly adjusted, etc.

Alternatively, the teacher may want to use a 'scarce' resource, such as a set of laptops, a digital camera or a scanner. All of these need to be carefully considered – do they need to be booked? Will somebody else be using this equipment at this time?

Contingency plans

What happens if it all goes horribly wrong? Although breakdowns with ICT are thankfully rare these days, there is always the possibility that a power cut or a network failure, or even a relatively minor problem such as a printer breaking down, can cause the lesson to go awry. The teacher needs to be prepared for this, and to have another activity or series of activities prepared in case the lesson cannot be started or completed due to technical reasons.

Planning for assessing ICT

This is perhaps the most challenging aspect of planning and preparing a lesson involving ICT. The type, place and purpose of the assessment will be determined by the nature of the lesson, for any assessment has to match the objectives and intended learning outcomes for that particular lesson.

Strategies for teaching ICT

Teaching interactively

An effective pedagogy in all teaching is the use of interactivity. Unless children are active participants in any lesson it could be argued that they are not learning. Learning occurs only when children are engaged, curious and challenged. In ICT interaction will be between: the child and the ICT task they are engaged in; the child and the teacher or other adult; and the child and his or her peers.

The provision of interactive ICT tasks

The level of interactivity in ICT tasks will depend on the software that has been selected, and the open-endedness of the activity. In Chapter 10 we discussed the need for software that can provide opportunities so that the children are in control of the computer, rather than the other way round. While some software may include characters from children's culture, be fast, noisy and 'fun', the educational value of these packages is usually minimal. Therefore careful selection is always necessary. In most cases it is the quality and management of the activity *you* devise that will be important. By using open-ended tasks children will be working at their own level, an important aspect of inclusive practice.

Consider how interactivity is being used in the ICT lesson below.

Case study

In this lesson the teacher has been teaching the children how to save their work, log off the computer, reboot the computer and relocate their work. She is using a collaborative and creative writing activity to consolidate the children's learning, and is teaching her whole class in the ICT suite.

The children are working in pairs and begin to write a story. After a few minutes, the teacher requests that the children save their work and log off their computer. She then moves the pairs around to other computers, where they reboot and locate the story left by the previous pair, and continue the story. After another few minutes, the teacher moves each pair onto a third computer. The children then return to the first computer that they used and complete the story. This collaborative approach to story-writing is at once both effective and powerful, and allows pupils of all abilities to participate in the activity. They can then finish the piece off, perhaps by adding images, borders and different font sizes and colours. They might be really ambitious and reorder the text on the screen. Depending on the number of pupils in the class, there could be as many as 15 different stories written by six or more different pupils!

One of the real advantages of this activity is that it can be organized and managed in a number of different ways according to the age and ability of the pupils, and to the nature of the task. If there is only one computer available, or only a few, then pairs of pupil can take it in turn to write a small amount of text each. Alternatively, the text can be emailed to a partner school anywhere in the English-speaking world (or, as a primary modern foreign languages activity, to the country of the target language), or posted onto a website with invitations to respond. This could either be children actually adding to the story online, or emailing suggestions to the school concerned. A panel of children in the home class could then decide which direction the story might take. This activity demonstrates that ICT can genuinely act as a focus for collaborative learning and also provide a value-added component at the same time.

Inclusive Practices

All classes have children for whom inclusive practices are needed. These could be children with special educational needs (SEN), English as an additional language (EAL), or those who are gifted or very able.

Children with SEN

Practices could vary from differentiated worksheets to the use of demonstration, tutorials and verbal explanations. In the case of children with SEN this might mean using specialized ICT hardware and software, or special settings as part of the software or the operating system. For example, for visually impaired children the screen image might be enlarged using the zoom or magnifying glass options.

When all children are working on computers, their individual physical needs also need to be considered. It is not only physically disabled children who may need tables and chairs at different heights, and monitors at different angles. All children should be working safely.

Consider Carl in that the case study below.

Case study

Carl is a Year 3 child with special educational needs. He and his class have been looking at how the use of adjectives can improve the quality of their written work, and now he and a teaching assistant are going to use the computer and word processing software to see how they can make 'the old house' (a noun phrase taken from the story Carl is presently writing) a little more inspiring.

In discussion with the teaching assistant Carl writes:

- The old, dark house
- The old, very dark house
- The old, dark, creepy house
- The old, dark and creepy house in the woods

So, it is not exactly Proust, is it? But it will improve the descriptive element of Carl's story.

It could be argued that this was just electronic typewriting, but in this activity Carl has been interacting with the computer, the software and an adult. He has had to:

- use his word processing skills to manipulate the words in his phrase, and to insert his new, descriptive writing into his original piece of writing
- discuss his choice of words, his spelling and his punctuation; and the teaching assistant has been scaffolding both his ICT skills and his English concepts.

> ### Case study (continues)
>
> At every step of the way this activity was child led, with the computer being used as a storage area for the pupil's ideas and efforts. Carl's relationship with the teaching assistant was also interactive, as it was based on collaboration. In their planning the teacher could alternatively have decided that Carl could have worked collaboratively with another child, and this would have enabled the children to scaffold for each other. The quality of discussion is crucial as they talk to each other to solve a problem. This articulation of ideas can produce some really high-level discussion in even the youngest children, developing higher order thinking skills such as reasoning and problem solving.

In this case study the inclusive practice experienced by Carl through the use of support and an open-ended task was effective. This model would be equally effective for other children.

When using a teaching assistant in these circumstances you must ensure that they have the appropriate skills, subject knowledge and teaching skills to support and scaffold competently. In cases where children have English as an additional language (EAL), a bilingual teaching assistant could be used.

Children with EAL

Children who have EAL could also use software with the alphabets and symbols of their home language. They could learn to locate and use online bilingual books. This would enable them use their skills at home (should there be a computer available) and to share books in their home language with other family members.

Children who are gifted or very able

When considering inclusive practices the use of collaborative, open-ended tasks will allow all children to work at their own level. In our earlier example of collaborative story-writing, there were many opportunities for enabling children to access higher levels of understanding. A more traditional story-writing activity could involve a teacher setting a theme, and the children responding individually. The more able children have the capability to write fluently and easily, perhaps without ever truly extending themselves. The less able children will consistently find this sort of task difficult. What cannot be denied is that the children become very expert at identifying exactly what the teacher is looking for and at writing for an audience of one person. However, with a collaborative element to the task, the children have a wider sense of audience, as their work will be read by their peers as well as the teacher – or even by adults or children in a distant location whom they do not know. This activity also develops children's higher order language skills. Apart from developing an appropriate sense of audience, it also develops reading for meaning and editing skills, as they need to be able to read what a previous writer has written, process it, and then subsequently develop it in a meaningful and sensible way.

With older and more able children, this could be further developed through what is termed 'transforming text'. This is where an original piece of text, such as a story, is transformed into another form, such as a newspaper report or a play script. If we consider the newspaper first, there are a number of higher order reading skills involved. The children will need to make the story more 'reportage' in style, with perhaps some significant changes to the structure and layout of the text. This would then provide the opportunity for some additional ICT key skill development: the children could cut and paste the text into a table on the page, perhaps with three columns and a large box at the top for the title. If the original story were to be transformed into a play script, then the teacher would need to ensure that there were at least two characters involved. Any speech marks would need to be removed, and the text would need to be reformatted so that each speaker would have their names located in the left-hand margin on the page, next to their lines. Description would need to be repositioned alongside the narrator or stage directions. Again, this is a good example of ICT key skills being developed alongside literacy skills.

Clearly these are powerful activities that are aimed at older or more able primary phase children. For younger children, an example activity might involve transforming a poem into a story, or vice-versa. Although it may be a simpler task, the principles are exactly the same.

The use of questioning

The use of effective questioning cannot be underestimated. As well as providing evidence of children's attainment of the learning outcomes, it also provides opportunities for the teacher to reinforce and extend children's learning through scaffolding and developing children's metacognitive strategies.

This can be done through the use of a range of open-ended yet focused questions. Example questions include:

- How many turtle steps do you think it will take to move the floor turtle forward and park it under that chair?
- How far will you have to move the turtle forward to join those two lines up?
- What would happen if you changed that angle from 40 degrees to 60 degrees? What would happen if you made that shape repeat 16 rather than 8 times?

Indeed, any question of the 'What would happen if...?', 'How far?', 'How many?' type should lead to the correct kind of response from the child. This open-ended questioning will make the children think carefully about the answer, and the act of thinking through and formulating an answer will reinforce and extend learning.

Assessing and monitoring progress in ICT

There are several key reasons why assessments of ICT should be made:

- to identify achievement and to indicate where children are in their understanding and skills in ICT
- to plan the next stage in children's ICT development and learning, thus ensuring continuity and progression
- to demonstrate children's progress against national targets
- to identify those children who may need 'catch-up' activities
- to help teachers to evaluate their own effectiveness, particularly in their teaching.

Assessment for learning is clearly the preferred method of assessing children where ICT is being used. However, in order for it to be effective, children need to:

- understand what the objectives, outcomes and assessment criteria are for a lesson
- identify the next steps in their learning and set their own targets for their ICT development
- have opportunities to talk about what they have learned and what they have found difficult, using the lesson objectives as a focus
- work and discuss together, focusing on how to improve their understanding and skills
- explain the steps in their thinking and use of hardware and software
- have time to reflect on their learning.

The involvement of the children in the assessment process ensures that any evidence collected will be representative of the work they have done, accurate and thorough. However, there is also the need to assess children summatively. This is usually done at the end of each academic year through teacher assessment, and at the end of both Key Stages through external assessment procedures. This generally means allocating a National Curriculum level: a difficult task, because the level descriptors for ICT are lengthy and contain elements from all aspects of ICT in the National Curriculum. The teacher will have to make a judgement about children's work by taking into account strengths and weaknesses in ICT over a period of time and in a range of contexts. It is not possible to allocate a level from a single piece of work, as this will not cover all the aspects of ICT as set out in each level description, but will only provide some evidence of attainment in one or two elements of a level description. The National Curriculum in Action website at www.ncaction.org.uk provides very good support in this difficult task, through the provision of examples of pupil work with descriptions and explanations as to why a particular piece of work has been assessed in the way that it has.

Accessing higher levels of learning and understanding

The time that has been saved by getting the computer to turn the data into information and then displaying it can be used to access higher levels of learning and understanding. This is where the skill of the teacher comes into focus, especially when asking open-ended questions. The teacher can pose a number of leading questions of a 'Why?' or 'What if...?' nature. This will extend children's thinking and thus their learning: instead of spending the time colouring in the bars on the graph, they now have to think through potentially complex problems to explain why they have got their results. Indeed, it is in this interpretation and evaluation phase of the lesson that the most powerful learning takes place – and this will have been facilitated by the use of ICT.

Conclusion

The intention of this chapter has been to deal with the practical aspects of teaching when using ICT in the primary school. The next chapter will deal with the role of ICT beyond the primary curriculum.

References

Department for Education and Employment (1998), *High Status, High Standards.* Circular Number 4/98: (Annex B). London: DfEE.

Websites

National Curriculum in Action www.ncaction.org.uk (Accessed April 2007.)
National Curriculum Online www.nc.uk.net (Accessed April 2007.)
QCA Assessment for Learning www.qca.org.uk/7658.html/ (Accessed April 2007.)
Schemes of Work www.standards.dfee.gov.uk/schemes (Accessed April 2007.)

 # Teaching Information and Communication Technology: Beyond the Curriculum

Nick Easingwood

WOW!

(Year 5 child's response to seeing the mould he had grown on cheese magnified on the digital microscope)

Introduction

We have already discussed the pedagogy, practicalities and possibilities that ICT can bring to the primary curriculum. Chapter 10 considered how modern technologies have enhanced everyday life, and the role that ICT can play in the school curriculum. Chapter 11 discussed how education in ICT can be delivered within the primary school and its curriculum. However, the power that ICT offers can be harnessed so that it is being used as much more than just a learning and teaching tool, or even as a subject in its own right. It offers wider possibilities, beyond the primary school classroom or ICT suite. As learning and teaching moves steadily away from the rigid constraints of the curriculum, the potential to use ICT creatively has developed.

One of the main features of education in England at the turn of the twenty-first century is the increasing flexibility of both schools and their curriculum. Gone are the days of the school opening at nine o'clock in the morning and closing at three thirty in the afternoon, with perhaps a lunchtime or after-school sports club or an educational visit as the only extras to the curriculum. Recent initiatives such as the introduction of pre-school breakfast and post-school homework clubs are just two examples of the significant evolution that primary education faces. Seminal documents from the British government such as *Every Child Matters* (DfES, 2004) and *Excellence and Enjoyment* (DfES, 2003), which have led to workforce reform and a move to cross-curricular teaching, have meant that the primary curriculum must become increasingly flexible to cope with these key initiatives. These, along with the widening curriculum and other themes such as inclusion, have ensured that the work of the primary school has to move beyond the classroom. ICT can play a significant role in delivering these initiatives.

ICT and the Every Child Matters agenda

As far as English schools are concerned, *Every Child Matters* is the most significant document to be published for many years. Arising from the Children Act of 2004, it connects children's services such as education, health and social services. Another key feature is the establishment of multi-agency working, with child-centred professionals located together in order to facilitate communication and effective practice.

The main tenet of the Act was to establish the child at the centre of the process through the establishment of five measurable outcomes. These are:

- stay safe
- be healthy
- enjoy and achieve
- achieve economic well-being
- make a positive contribution.

The *Every Child Matters* document underpins everything that happens in English schools, so teachers need to be aware of the above five points, and consider carefully how they might impact on their practice in teaching and using ICT.

Stay safe

Meeting the requirements for every child to stay safe is probably the most important and the easiest of the five aspects to achieve using ICT. It takes two main forms: safety in the classroom, and safety online.

Safety in the classroom

Providing a safe environment for children and staff at all times is a fundamental requirement for all schools. Although all electrical equipment is subject to an annual safety check by a qualified person, both the ICT subject leader and the class teacher should make regular safety checks on all hardware whenever it is to be used. A regular risk assessment should be completed and included as part of the lesson plan. Aspects to consider include:

- ensuring that all health and safety regulations are closely adhered to and regularly reviewed
- checking that there are no trailing cables that could provide a trip hazard
- checking that there is no chafing or wear on cables that could give the user an electric shock, or even lead to electrocution
- making sure that all cables are properly plugged in to wall sockets and computers
- ensuring that there is an emergency plan if anything should go wrong. This might include where to go for help or first aid in the event of an accident, or how to report instances of 'cyber-bullying'.

Safety online

Much has been said and written in the media and elsewhere about the potential dangers of children using the internet. While it is certainly true that these dangers can exist, they should not prevent the teacher from using this significant resource with their classes. The advantages far outweigh the potential disadvantages, which can be eliminated if a few simple precautions are taken.

It is essential for the school to have an Acceptable Use Policy (AUP) in place. This is a completely separate document from the school ICT policy, in that it specifically refers to teaching and learning using the internet. As the name implies, it is directly concerned with establishing clear protocols and guidelines for how the internet and email should be used in schools, with clear sanctions for those who do not use it correctly. This might include temporary withdrawal of user access or even, in the most extreme cases, suspension or expulsion from the school. Although this is unlikely to happen in the primary phase, the facility needs to exist for those children who may download illegal material, who use the internet and email as a means of cyber bullying or harassment, or who use ICT to interfere with other people's computer systems (often known as 'hacking', this is illegal under the Computer Misuse Act of 1990).

An AUP includes a permission slip that has to be signed by parent/guardians and returned to the school before children are allowed to use the internet or email. This gives the school the right to withdraw errant children from using this facility, and also protects the school if a child does download anything that is illegal, whether by accident or by design.

The school can of course take a number of other precautions to ensure that the internet is used safely and correctly. These include:

- Ensuring that all staff know procedures for keeping children safe, and are able to effectively communicate these to them. This requires regular staff training to include aspects such as making sure children do not put personal details on websites or in emails, and teaching the children how to protect themselves (for instance, by reporting instances of cyber bullying, and being able to spot material that is illegal or biased).
- Establishing a safe online environment through the use of a secure area. This is set up by staff and only allows access to those websites which have been 'vetted' in advance. It could also include blocking or restricting the use of chat rooms and forums. This is where a virtual learning environment (VLE) will be particularly useful, as only those children who are assigned to it by the teacher will be able to access it.

Be healthy

Health and safety is a critically important consideration for all schools. As far as using computers is concerned, there are several important issues to consider. Hardware is designed for use by adults rather than by children, and as such is adult sized. Therefore the teacher needs to ensure that:

- Monitors and screens are positioned so that there is no glare from lights or sunlight on them, which will make them difficult to read. Blinds may need to be fitted and drawn.
- Children are correctly seated in front of the screen; this means that their eyes should be level with the top of the illuminated area of the screen, and their hands and wrists should be supported. Where possible, proper operators' chairs should be used. These are adjustable for both height and posture, and have five feet to prevent them from tipping over. This can be particularly difficult with young children where they may have to be raised when using adult-sized monitors, or when laptops are being used.
- Wrist support may be necessary to prevent repetitive strain injuries. The teacher also needs to consider whether some alternative input device might be useful, especially for those children who are very young or who have special needs. An adult-sized mouse can be very difficult for a young child to control and manipulate, so laptops with tracker pads or tracker balls may be preferable.
- There is plenty of room for the children to work away from the computers, including work tables.
- If possible, air conditioning is fitted.
- The data projector and whiteboard, screen or interactive whiteboard are positioned so that the user is not blinded by the light or reflective glare from the screens.

Enjoy and achieve

There is a great deal of evidence to indicate that ICT can significantly enhance pupil motivation and self-esteem. The Impact2 (2002) project indicated that those schools that make extensive use of ICT achieved higher results than those that did not. It could be argued that these former schools are enlightened enough to see the importance of ICT, and use it effectively to enhance practice.

It is incumbent on the teacher to ensure that all activities that are set for children are appropriately challenging, creative, imaginative and suitable for their given age and ability. This includes children who are part of the inclusion agenda, and those with individual education plans.

As a consequence of this requirement, schools will need to have sufficient quantities of a wide range of current hardware and software. There is also a necessity for all staff, including teachers and teaching assistants, to be highly trained and skilled in the use of ICT from both a technical and pedagogical perspective. There should be a deeply established culture of ICT in the school, not only for teaching and learning, but also for administrative tasks such as registers, newsletters and labels for wall displays, as well as regular communication to parents via a school website, email and texts. All school policies and schemes of work should contain appropriate references to a type of ICT that is deeply embedded into the curriculum and school life in general.

Achieve economic well-being

At first glance this might perhaps appear to be the most difficult to achieve with primary phase children, given that they are not being prepared for the world of work at this age. However, the National Curriculum for England provides several opportunities to address this. We have already seen that the tone of the ICT document is geared towards developing ICT capability, and key phrases include terms such as 'analyse', 'reflect' and 'evaluate'. This might include directly connecting to work involving control technology, where the children can discuss where technology is used to control aspects that effect children's lives, such as traffic lights or automatic doors in shops and supermarkets. Children need to be taught to think carefully about these and learn to apply them to their work. Freedman (2005) highlights several other activities that can be included here, such as:

- understanding why it is important to be computer literate
- using online learning to ensure that all can access education
- using the internet to learn about other cultures and societies
- learning how to set up websites of their own
- debating and evaluating the effects of technology on the environment

- considering key aspects of ICT law such as copyright and data protection
- evaluating different types of electronic data and information.

Make a positive contribution

This is concerned with allowing children to make a positive contribution not only during lessons, but also beyond the classroom. It might include children contributing via the internet and email in a manner that enhances teaching and learning: perhaps through participating in an online discussion in a virtual learning environment. They will of course need to be taught *how* to participate in such forums to ensure that they follow the generally accepted protocols. Activities might include collaborating with other schools, either in their own country or abroad (especially useful with modern foreign languages), and considering the differences in use of technology within their own and other countries.

Children could be involved in working collaboratively with their peers on ICT-based projects such as website design, film-making through digital video-editing, using presentation software, or using the interactive whiteboard to show the other members of the class specific findings.

Using ICT to support cross-curricular learning and teaching

Cross-curricular learning and teaching will be particularly important when the modern foreign languages initiative is implemented in 2010. *Excellence and Enjoyment: A Strategy for Primary Schools* (DfES, 2003) was published as a response to the growing feeling that there was too great an emphasis on literacy and mathematics in English primary schools. This document intended to give greater emphasis to schools being able to design their own delivery of the statutory curriculum, and place more emphasis on the Foundation subjects, which had been 'squeezed out' in recent years. One of the main themes was the return to a cross-curricular style of learning and teaching.

Effective teachers have always been able to deliver all aspects of the curriculum in a cross-curricular way. Indeed, it could be argued that the only way to deliver the entire requirements of the National Curriculum is to teach in a completely integrated manner.

Children have always learned at least as much out of the school as in it, and the introduction of modern technologies has significantly narrowed the gap between learning in and out of school. We have already discussed in the previous two chapters the role that ICT plays both as a discrete subject and as a means of supporting other subjects, and how this can be delivered.

The use of interactive whiteboards

One of the most exciting innovations to be used in classrooms is the interactive whiteboard (IWB). This is a useful tool for delivering all aspects of the curriculum (except, curiously, ICT), but is ideal for teaching in a cross-curricular way. One of the main advantages of the IWB is that it can be used as the centrepiece for whole class lessons, or for group teaching by the teacher, teaching assistant and, of course, the children.

An IWB can be mounted on a wall or put on a stand that can be moved on wheels. It is connected to a computer via a cable, which in turn is connected to a data projector that projects the computer's images onto the whiteboard. Depending on the type of board that is being used, the user touches the image on the whiteboard to provoke a response from the software or hardware as appropriate. This can be done either by hand, or with a special, penlike device called a stylus. The real flexibility comes with the fact that it can be used as a display screen, an electronic flip-chart, or as a resource base for all areas of the curriculum.

One of the most commonly used software packages includes three basic modes:

- Desktop mode – this is where the IWB is effectively used as an alternative input device that can be seen by all members of the class or a group. The user points and clicks on the board, which provokes a response from the hardware and software. This is particularly useful for demonstrating how to use pieces of software.
- Annotate over windows mode – although similar to the mode above, this is where the user can write or draw over a standard desktop, or whatever the computer is displaying at the time, without being able to access any of the features of the software. This is particularly useful for highlighting key features of software or for emphasizing key teaching points, perhaps by highlighting text in a word processed document or presentation. This can include lines, arrows and highlights.
- Flipchart mode – this is the most powerful use of the IWB and is the one that is most likely to be used in the normal course of events. This is where the user writes or draws on it in the same way as they would on a more traditional whiteboard or flip chart. The user can employ a range of tools to assist in the teaching process. This includes the ability to draw lines of different thicknesses and colours, graphics, shapes and grids, as well as text and handwriting. The software even offers the facility to convert freehand writing into a standard computer font! One of the most useful resources are the backgrounds, a range of pre-prepared screens such as countryside scenes, board games, maps, sports fields and courts (such as football and rugby pitches and tennis courts), musical staves, handwriting page templates, clock faces and graphs. All of these can be used and drawn over using the various writing and drawing facilitie,s making this mode ideal for all sorts of primary school activities.

There is little doubt that the IWB is a remarkable technological development that has the power to transform the way that pupils are taught and learn. It brings learning to life in a manner that is very visual. However, a necessary word of caution here. As with all ICT resources, the teacher needs to consider carefully how and when the IWB is used. It should not be used simply because it is there: there has to be an appropriate pedagogy employed at all times. In other words, as with all aspects of ICT, it will be at its most effective as a learning and teaching resource when it provides opportunities that simply would not be possible without it. The teacher needs to be able to exercise this professional judgement before using it.

Certainly, it could be argued that much of what it offers could be done with an old-fashioned overhead projector, pens and clear film: but this would not offer the flexibility. As the name suggests, the key to the IWB is the ability to be interactive. All can use it and the results can then be saved and recalled for further work at a later time. Individualized word lists or tables can be produced and recalled for later use; the board can provide the focus for whole class or group use and can stimulate a wide range of learning and teaching situations with children across the primary age range.

The IWB is particularly effective with younger pupils. For example, in a mathematics lesson involving shape and space, the teacher might begin by drawing a Venn diagram and some shapes on the board, with the children then sorting the shapes depending on their properties before dragging and dropping them into the appropriate part of the diagram. Alternatively, the user can draw shapes on the board and then transform them by 'rubber banding' them into new shapes and positions in the same way that the more traditional pin board was used. These facilities provide a great deal of stimulation, particularly as a starter to a lesson.

ICT beyond the classroom

One of the main advantages of ICT is the fact that it can be used in a number of remote locations, perhaps through wireless network connections. This flexibility, which has been taken for granted in the world of commerce and industry, is now available to primary schools. Many schools are now purchasing laptops with this facility, so children can connect to the internet or each other in the classroom, school hall or even on the playground or school field. One of the paradoxes of technological progress is that the ICT that started with one computer in the corner of the classroom, and then progressed to a specialist ICT suite, has now returned to support classroom-based activities and learning beyond the classroom. This means that children now have access to the full power of ICT within their own school environment and beyond. If they go on a school trip, the class set of laptops can be taken too. If museums and galleries are visited, it is possible that there will be open-access wireless network connections. This means that while on their visit children can access the facility's website or other websites containing related material, or they can email experts to ask focused questions about what they are looking at.

Using museums and galleries as learning environments

It is important to appreciate that even in this highly technological age, there is never any substitute for children experiencing the 'real thing'. An educational visit to a museum or gallery is always an extremely worthwhile activity. This is because it provides the children with the opportunity to actually see and compare real and often famous artefacts with images that they may have seen in books or other media. Often, the real thing does not always match up to the popular impression. For example, Leonardo da Vinci's famous painting of the Mona Lisa is much smaller than most people imagine, and is displayed in the Louvre in Paris behind bulletproof glass. Similarly, Stephenson's Rocket, displayed in the National Railway Museum in York, is far removed from the bright yellow and shiny steam locomotive that is the popular image of an early steam train. It is small and black and very much looking its age. It is important to ensure that children have the opportunity to have a highly focused, structured visit, often under the guidance of experts, rather than as casual browsers.

It may be tempting to use ICT to simulate first-hand, practical experience: but this should be resisted at all costs. The wide range of DVDs, videos, websites and CD-ROMs that are available are of variable quality, and seldom replicate the real thing adequately. However, if properly utilized, ICT can enhance the learning experience whether it is inside or outside of the classroom. It is much more beneficial to use ICT to enhance an educational visit in a way that is both interesting and imaginative. The kind of ICT-based activities that might be employed here include:

- Using the internet to research the artefacts that the children are going to see in a museum. This will give the children background information in advance of the visit, so when actually seeing the object concerned for real, they will understand more about it. This might even include taking a virtual tour of the key galleries to be visited.
- Using the venue's website to find out any costs associated with the trip (such as entrance fees), which could then be modelled in a spreadsheet.
- Using the venue's website to plan the route of the visit and to identify key artefacts and displays to be viewed. This is particularly important in a large museum, such as the Natural History, Science or British Museums in London. These cannot be seen in their entirety in a single day, so it is necessary to look at the key features that are directly related to the theme that is being studied.
- Using digital cameras to record what is seen in the venue.
- After the visit, creating a website or interactive presentation based around their visit. This might include a multimedia presentation using images, sounds and music to illustrate and further explain what they have seen. Information could be inserted into the presentation and hyperlinked to a range of other illustrative resources. This might include still or film images of the object when it was in use contained in a website, or commentary by those who may have used it.

Home–school links: the use of virtual learning environments

A more recent development of ICT now used in the educational context is the virtual learning environment (VLE). This is a web-based piece of software that allows teachers to deliver content to children via the internet. It contains a number of features, many of which are already pre-existing, collected together in one secure place to provide a means of online delivery. This includes a discussion forum, instant messaging, the means to post content online easily, and a way of enabling children to respond. It also includes the facility to share and download files and information. The teacher can create content, post it online and the children can respond to it in a number of ways. This content might be a question for discussion, a task for the children or a quiz. It might involve the children submitting work electronically via the VLE for marking by the teacher, or the pupils and the teacher interacting with each other via the use of a discussion board or a forum. Alternatively, the teacher might set them an online quiz, which the children respond to by writing the correct answer or ticking a 'yes' or 'no' box. The software can then automatically collate and mark the answers and present this information in a number of ways.

The recent move towards setting homework for primary-aged children can be facilitated by the use of a VLE. The children can follow up work completed in the classroom through the use of the VLE. This might include submitting work online, or discussing what they have been doing in school with their classmates or the teacher. Indeed, their parents might be encouraged to participate in a live chat session, creating closer home–school links. The VLE could be utilized within the school day, but would probably be more useful when the children are located away from each other, such as when they are at home or in a homework club.

Conclusion

The purpose of this chapter was to illustrate the role that ICT can have in developing the curriculum beyond the classroom. The implementation of many initiatives (such as Every Child Matters and Excellence and Enjoyment) have extended and enhanced English primary schools in a way that was unthinkable even five years ago. The notion of extended schools and the integration of the education system with other local authority services has had a profound effect upon the way that primary children are taught and learn. Fortunately, the development of a wide range of ICT resources (such as IWBs and VLEs) can assist greatly in the implementation of these initiatives. The power that ICT brings to teaching and learning through its capability to be interactive can enable teachers to rise quickly and effectively to the challenges created by these new initiatives.

References

Department for Education and Skills (2002), *Languages for All: Languages for Life*. London: DfES.

Department for Education and Skills (2003), *Excellence and Enjoyment: A Strategy for Primary Schools*. London: DfES.

Department for Education and Skills (2004), *Every Child Matters: Change for Children*. London: DfES.

Freedman, T. (2005), *Every Child Matters: What It Means for the ICT Teacher*. www.ictineducation.org (Accessed May 2007.)

Impact2 (2002) Report partners.becta.org.uk/index.php?section=rh&rid=11218 (Accessed May 2007.)

Recommended Websites

English

BookBox www.channel4learning.net/sites/bookbox/home.htm

Children's Creative www.childrenscreative.com/

Literacy Activity Builder www.ngfl-cymru.org.uk/vtc-home/vtc-ks1-home/vtc-ks1-english(2)/lab_-_ks1_-_eng.htm

Talk Dog www.bteducation.org/img/lib/talkdog/talkdog.shtml

Giggle Poetry www.gigglepoetry.com/

Mathematics

Count On www.counton.org/

Interactive Teaching Programs www.standards.dfes.gov.uk/primary/publications/mathematics/itps/

NumberGym www.numbergym.co.uk/

Nrich http://nrich.maths.org/public/

Rainforest Maths www.rainforestmaths.com/

Science

Planet-Science www.planet-science.com/home.html

Science Essentials www.channel4learning.net/sites/essentials/science/index.shtml

Science Clips www.bbc.co.uk/schools/scienceclips/index_flash.shtml

The Virtual Body www.ehc.com/vbody.asp

The Yuckiest Site on the Internet http://yucky.discovery.com/flash/

ICT

Becta www.becta.org.uk/

NAACE Primary www.mape.org.uk/

ICTopus www.ictopus.org.uk/

ICTeachers www.icteachers.co.uk/

Learning and Teaching Using ICT http://samples.lgfl.org.uk/primary/

Index